© 2000
Text copyright by Selwyn Hughes
All rights reserved
Printed in the United States of America

0–8054–2323–0

Published by Broadman & Holman Publishers, Nashville, Tennessee
Editorial Team: Leonard G. Goss, John Landers
Cover & Interior Design: Identity Design Inc., Dallas, Texas

Dewey Decimal Classification: 242.2
Subject Heading: DEVOTIONAL EXERCISES

Every Day Light™
CWR, Waverley Abbey House, Waverley Lane, Farnham, Surrey GU9 8EP

EDL Classic, *Life's Greatest Purpose* Text 1998 © Selwyn Hughes
Material taken from *Every Day with Jesus* Discovering Life's Greatest Purpose 1983
Revised edition in this format 1998 © Selwyn Hughes

Unless otherwise indicated, all Scripture references are from the Holy Bible,
New International Version (NIV) Copyright © 1973, 1978, 1984 by the International Bible Society.
Other references are marked as follows: GNB, Good News Bible: The Bible in Today's English Version,
© American Bible Society 1966, 1971, 1976, used by permission; RSV, Revised Standard Version
of the Bible, copyrighted 1946, 1952, © 1971, 1973; *The Message*, the New Testament
in Contemporary English, © 1993 by Eugene H. Peterson, published by NavPress,
Colorado Springs, Colo.; TLB, The Living Bible, copyright © Tyndale House Publishers,
Wheaton, Ill., 1971, used by permission.

AUSTRALIA: CMC Australasia
P.O. Box 519, Belmont, Victoria 3216 Tel: (03) 5241 3288

CANADA: CMC Distribution Ltd.
P.O. Box 7000, Niagara on the Lake, Ontario L0S 1J0 Tel: 1 800 325 1297

INDIA: Full Gospel Literature Stores
254 Kilpauk Garden Road, Chennai 600010 Tel: (44) 644 3073

KENYA: Keswick Bookshop
P.O. Box 10242, Nairobi Tel: (02) 331692/226047

MALAYSIA: Salvation Book Centre (M)
23 Jalan SS2/64, Sea Park, 47300 Petaling Jaya, Selangor Tel: (3) 7766411

NEW ZEALAND: CMC New Zealand Ltd.
P.O. Box 949, 205 King Street South, Hastings
Tel: (6) 8784408, Toll free: 0800 333639

NIGERIA: FBFM, (Every Day with Jesus)
Prince's Court, 37 Ahmed Onibudo Street, P.O. Box 70952, Victoria Island
Tel: 01 2617721, 616832, 4700218

REPUBLIC OF IRELAND: Scripture Union
40 Talbot Street, Dublin 1 Tel: (01) 8363764

SINGAPORE: Campus Crusade Asia Ltd.
315 Outram Road, 06–08 Tan Boon Liat Building, Singapore 169074
Tel: (65) 222 3640

SOUTH AFRICA: Struik Christian Books (Pty Ltd)
P.O. Box 193, Maitland 7405, Cape Town Tel: (021) 551 5900

SRI LANKA: Christombu Investments
27 Hospital Street, Colombo 1 Tel: (1) 433142/328909

USA: CMC Distribution
P.O. Box 644, Lewiston, New York 14092–0644 Tel: 1 800 325 1297

# QUIET TIME

Jesus, today place me
fully aware
in this world I live in,
so loud and confusing—
full of clashing beauty
and corruption.

This world you loved
so much you
gave your life for it.
Your world.

Love it through
me, Jesus!

© Susan Lenzkes

Signature Series

SELWYN HUGHES

# DISCOVERING LIFE'S GREATEST PURPOSE

Every Day Light for Your Journey

BROADMAN
&HOLMAN
PUBLISHERS

NASHVILLE, TENNESSEE

# WEEK 1

## WHAT IS GOD'S HIGHEST PURPOSE FOR OUR LIVES?

It is good to remember:
God created me.
His creation gives me worth.
God loves me.
His love gives me belonging.
God planned for me.
His plan gives me
significance.
God gifted me.
His gifts give me competence.
Christ died for me.
His sacrifice makes me completely
acceptable to God.
It is when we are forgiven much
that we love much.

# G O D — L E T  M E  B E  A W A R E

"Dear friends, let us love one another, for love comes from God. Everyone who loves has been born of God and knows God. Whoever does not love does not know God, because God is love. This is how God showed his love among us: He sent his one and only Son into the world that we might live through him. This is love: not that we loved God, but that he loved us and sent his Son as an atoning sacrifice for our sins. *Dear friends, since God so loved us, we also ought to love one another.* No one has ever seen God; but if we love each other, God lives in us and his love is made complete in us."

1 John 4:7–12

We set out in this edition to explore a theme of unparalleled importance—*discovering life's greatest purpose.* Have you ever asked yourself the question: Why am I here? What am I doing in this world? What is the purpose of my existence? If you feel that much of your life is purposeless, let me assure you right away that God does have a purpose for your life—a high and noble purpose. As you discover it in the weeks that lie ahead, it will move your life into a completely new dimension.

## Life's Greatest Purpose

What, then, is life's greatest purpose? This: *to be aware*

*of God and aware of others.* I am going to assume that you are already aware of God, so the question I want to put to you today is this: How aware are you of others? Do you care for those who are pressed down with deep, perplexing problems? Have you a genuine concern for people in trouble? God's highest priority in this universe has to do with *people.* He is interested in things, of course—He created them—but His primary concern is for people. "For God so loved the world that he gave his one and only Son, that whoever believes in him shall not perish but have eternal life" (John 3:16).

If we are to discover and develop God's greatest purpose for our lives, then we must bring our concern in line with His concern. One great thinker said, "Most human problems stem from the fact that we treat people as things and things as people." Put your hand in the hand of God. Realize that God's highest interest is in people. Decide now to make God's priority your priority; and make people—not things—your primary concern.

My Father and my God, if people are
Your priority, then help me to make them
my priority, too. Help me to invest my greatest
energy not in things, but in people.
God, make me aware, for Jesus' sake. Amen.

God's highest interest is in people.

# A UNIVERSAL CRAVING

"I consider everything a loss compared to the surpassing greatness of knowing Christ Jesus my Lord, for whose sake I have lost all things. I consider them rubbish, that I may gain Christ and be found in him, not having a righteousness of my own that comes from the law, but that which is through faith in Christ—the righteousness that comes from God and is by faith. I want to know Christ and the power of his resurrection and the fellowship of sharing in his sufferings, becoming like him in his death, and so, somehow, to attain to the resurrection from the dead. Not that I have already obtained all this, or have already been made perfect, but I press on to take hold of that for which Christ Jesus took hold of me."

## Philippians 3:8–12

As we begin to open up our theme of discovering life's greatest purpose, we remind ourselves that because God's highest purposes in this universe have to do with people, then we must bring our purpose in line with His purpose. We can do that by determining to make people, more than things, our greatest priority.

## The Purpose of Existence

Every human being carries an innate desire to know the

purpose of his existence. Listen to what Dr. William Sheldon says about this deep, elemental desire in the human heart: "Continued observations . . . lead almost inevitably to the conclusion that deeper and more fundamental than sexuality, deeper than the craving for social power, deeper even than the desire for possessions, there is a still more generalized craving in the human make-up. *It is the craving for the knowledge of the right direction.*" Every system of philosophy, whether religious or not, is really a human attempt to satisfy the craving to be pointed in the right direction.

A Christian need not be in any doubt about the direction in which God wants him to go and what is the Creator's highest purpose for his life. *It is receiving God's love, and then channeling that love into the lives of those around us who are weak and wounded.* God wants you to be a caring person, sensitive to the needs of others and aware of the way in which He wants you to minister to them. Whatever else God may have for you to do in this world, His highest purpose is to make you a channel of His tender, loving care to others. Once you grasp this, then you are on your way to fulfilling your highest destiny.

O Father, drive this truth deep into my spirit. Help me to see that I am on this earth for a high and noble purpose, and make that purpose more clear to me day by day. For Jesus' sake. Amen.

God wants you to be a caring person.

# A CHRISTIAN—
# ONE WHO CARES

"There are many parts, but one body. The eye cannot say to the hand, 'I don't need you!' And the head cannot say to the feet, 'I don't need you!' On the contrary, those parts of the body that seem to be weaker are indispensable, and the parts that we think are less honorable we treat with special honor. And the parts that are unpresentable are treated with special modesty, while our presentable parts need no special treatment. But God has combined the members of the body and has given greater honor to the parts that lacked it, so that there should be no division in the body, but that its parts should have equal concern for each other."

## 1 Corinthians 12:20–25

We ended yesterday by saying that God has a high and noble purpose for each one of us, but His *highest* purpose is that we might be the channel of His love to others. Every person needs to discover a reason for his or her life—the purpose for his or her presence on the earth, for without a purpose life becomes merely existence.

## God's Purpose for Christians

Peter, in his sermon on the day of Pentecost, said, "Save yourselves from this untoward generation" (Acts 2:40 KJV). The root meaning of the word *untoward* is "crooked," but it can also be translated "purposeless." The generation in which Peter lived wasn't going anywhere—it was adrift. That purposeless generation ended up making a sudden decision to crucify Jesus. It had no overall purpose, and thus was easily overtaken by a sudden and sinister purpose.

If we do not have a life purpose—a clear reason for being here in this world, then life becomes jaded. Without a purpose we are like sand dunes that are shifted and shaped by the prevailing wind. A Christian who does not see his or her life purpose in terms of what God wants him or her to achieve in this world will soon be overtaken by other purposes. Baron Von Huegel, a Roman Catholic layman, once gave this penetrating definition of a Christian: "A Christian is one who cares." How caring are you? Today you might rub shoulders with someone who is ready to come apart at the seams—but unless you are deeply sensitive, you might never notice it. All around us people are crying out to be loved, but many of us pursue our own desires with little or no understanding of the marvelous purpose that God has for us—to lift the fallen, cheer the fainthearted, and give hope to the hopeless.

O Father, as I come face to face with the highest reason
for my existence, help me not to turn from it, afraid
of the responsibility, but to embrace it, for by doing so,
I know I shall be walking with destiny. Amen.

Without a purpose, life becomes merely existence.

# A GOD WHO CARES

"Therefore, since we have been justified through faith, we have peace with God through our Lord Jesus Christ, through whom we have gained access by faith into this grace in which we now stand. And we rejoice in the hope of the glory of God. Not only so, but we also rejoice in our sufferings, because we know that suffering produces perseverance; perseverance, character; and character, hope. And hope does not disappoint us, because God has poured out his love into our hearts by the Holy Spirit, whom he has given us. *You see, at just the right time, when we were still powerless, Christ died for the ungodly.*"

Romans 5:1–6

We are seeing that the greatest purpose of our lives here on earth is to develop a deep and sensitive awareness towards others and demonstrate personal care for their pressing needs. "A Christian is one who cares," we said. Is this just mere rhetoric, or does it have a basis in fact? It is based on the greatest fact of the universe—the Creator cares.

## What God Is Really Like

A missionary addressing an audience in Madras, India, told them that the ultimate in caring is the picture of God upon a cross. He said, "The God we see in Jesus is a God who cares—cares enough to give Himself on a cross." After he had finished, the chairman, a Hindu doctor, arose and said,

"We appreciate this moving address, but we must not involve God in the affairs of this world. He is lifted above all these things. We must not humanize God."

In other words, God to him was a God who didn't care. But a God who doesn't care, doesn't count. The God who would sit in awful isolation, separated from the problems and difficulties of His creation, is not worth considering. I couldn't have respect for a God like that, and neither, I imagine, could you. But despite the statement of the Hindu doctor that "we must not involve God in the affairs of this world," the Almighty has, by His own volition, entered through the door of humanity and involved Himself with us in the person of His Son, Jesus Christ. As Edward Shillito put it in *Jesus of the Scars:*

> "The other gods were strong, but Thou became weak.
> They rose, but Thou didst stagger, to a throne.
> But to our wounds, only God's wounds can speak,
> And not a god has wounds but Thou alone."

O Father, I see so clearly that You are a God who cares—really cares. And because You care, I must care too. Help me become a truly caring person. For Jesus' sake. Amen.

A God who doesn't care, doesn't count.

# THE LAW
# OF CHRIST

"Then they came to Jericho. As Jesus and his disciples, together with a large crowd, were leaving the city, a blind man, Bartimaeus (that is, the Son of Timaeus), was sitting by the roadside begging. When he heard that it was Jesus of Nazareth, he began to shout, 'Jesus, Son of David, have mercy on me!' Many rebuked him and told him to be quiet, but he shouted all the more, 'Son of David, have mercy on me!' *Jesus stopped and said, 'Call him.'*"

## Mark 10:46–49

We continue meditating on the theme: *discovering life's greatest purpose.* We said yesterday that God is a God who cares. One scientist said, "The evidences of a caring God are seen everywhere in His creation; in the way the sun rises and sets, in the seasons of the earth, in the opening of a flower . . . all these shout to us that at the back of creation is a God who cares." The more closely we get to know God, the more caring we shall be. It is inevitable.

## Jesus' Interest

In the story of the blind man before us today, it is interesting to observe that before Jesus noticed the man, the people had little or no interest in him. Their response to his plea for Jesus to help him was: "Shut up!" (v. 48 TLB). When, however, Jesus said, "Tell him to come here," they rushed over to him and said, "Come on, he's calling you" (v. 49 TLB). Now Jesus' interest became their interest.

Something similar must happen to us. Although by nature we might not be caring people, we must live in such a close relationship with Jesus Christ that His concerns become our concerns, His sensitivity becomes our sensitivity, His interests become our interests. The Scripture says in Galatians 6:2 that we should "bear one another's burdens, and so fulfil the *law of Christ*" (RSV). When I first read this verse many years ago, I asked myself: What does it mean—the *law* of Christ? There are many laws which God has established in this universe—the law of gravity, the law of thermodynamics and so on—but none of them are of such high priority that they are called the law of Christ. I came to the conclusion, after thinking about it for some time, that the law of Christ is the law of caring. It is the law *par excellence.* Without it the universe would fall apart.

O God, help me to love by the law of Christ— the law of caring. Time is too short, and living too serious, to have any higher priority. This I ask in Jesus' name. Amen.

Bear one another's burdens.

# THE SECOND INCARNATION

"On the evening of that first day of the week, when the disciples were together, with the doors locked for fear of the Jews, Jesus came and stood among them and said, 'Peace be with you!' After he said this, he showed them his hands and side. The disciples were overjoyed when they saw the Lord. Again Jesus said, 'Peace be with you! *As the Father has sent me, I am sending you.*' And with that he breathed on them and said, 'Receive the Holy Spirit. If you forgive anyone his sins, they are forgiven; if you do not forgive them, they are not forgiven.'"

## John 20:19–21

We have been seeing over the past few days that the greatest model we have for caring is none other than the Almighty God Himself. We saw also that when Christ was here on earth, He, too, demonstrated a loving concern for people. It was said of Him that He "went around doing good and healing all who were under the power of the devil, because God was with him" (Acts 10:38).

## Jesus Is Living in His Church

Now, of course, Christ is no longer personally present on the earth, for after His death and resurrection, He returned to His Father in heaven. He has moved—but not without leaving a forwarding address! The New Testament teaches that today Christ can be seen and found in the words and loving deeds of His disciples—you and me. Someone has daringly called this extension of Christ's care and compassion, as expressed through the lives of His followers, "the second incarnation." Just as in the first incarnation, God came in the person of His Son, Jesus Christ, to show humanity that He cared, so in the second incarnation (His divine indwelling in His church), He is present in the world to spell out that same wondrous message—God cares.

I referred earlier to Baron Von Huegel's definition of a Christian as someone who cares. Someone asked him to define the church, and he gave this as the answer: "A society that cares." When a YMCA official was asked about the secret of the organization's success, he said, "We see a need, we pray about it and we do something about it." The climate in today's church, generally speaking, is: we see a need, we pray about it, we discuss it. We open our churches one day a week to have a religious service instead of opening them seven days a week as a service to all who are in need.

Gracious, loving heavenly Father, forgive us
that we are so long on words, but so short on
action. Help Your church to lead the way
in showing the world that You care.
For Your own dear name's sake. Amen.

Christ can be seen and found in . . . you and me.

W  E  E  K  **D A Y 7**  O  N  E

# LIFE IS SENSITIVITY

"When the Son of Man comes in his glory, and all the angels with him, he will sit on his throne . . . All the nations will be gathered before him, and he will separate the people from one another as a shepherd separates the sheep from the goats. He will put the sheep on his right and the goats on his left. Then the King will say to those on his right, 'Come, you who are blessed by my Father; take your inheritance, the kingdom prepared for you since the creation of the world. *For I was hungry and you gave me something to eat,* I was thirsty and you gave me something to drink, I was a stranger and you invited me in, I needed clothes and you clothed me, I was sick and you looked after me, *I was in prison and you came to visit me.'"*

## Matthew 25:31–36

During this week, we have been asking ourselves the question: What is God's highest purpose for our lives? The answer, we have seen, is to care for others as God cares for us and to be a channel of His love to those in need.

## Jesus in the Need of the Needy

Today we ask ourselves: How sensitive and alert are we to the needs of those around us? Someone has defined life as "sensitivity." This is an interesting definition, for when we examine life in all its aspects, we find that the lowest form of life is sensitive only to itself. The higher one rises in the scale of existence, the wider the range of sensitivity. Human beings, for example, have a wider range of sensitivity than animals; animals have a wider range of sensitivity than plant life, and so on. When you rise to the highest level of life ever demonstrated on this earth—the life of Jesus—you find total sensitivity. He said in today's passage, "I was hungry and you gave me something to eat . . . sick and you looked after me . . . in prison and you came to visit me." The righteous asked, "When?" He replied, "Whatever you did for one of the least of these brothers of mine, you did for me" (vv. 35–40). He was hungry in their hunger, bound in their imprisonment.

The person who defined life as "sensitivity" went on to say, "You can tell how high you have risen in the scale of life by asking yourself the question: How widely and how deeply do I care?" The person who said that the world would be a wonderful place if it weren't for people, revealed by that remark the depth of his own insensitivity. As we have been saying over the past week—a Christian is one who cares. Can this be said of you?

O God, my gracious Father, I want to live deeply and fully. I need a baptism of caring love to flow in and through my personality, for otherwise I shall be out of harmony with the eternal realities. Amen.

How widely and how deeply do I care?

Strength is for service, not status. Each of us needs to look after the good of the people around us, asking ourselves: "How can I help?" That's exactly what Jesus did. He didn't make it easy for himself by avoiding people's troubles, but waded right in and helped out.

Romans 15:1–3, from *The Message*
— Eugene Peterson

# THE CHURCH
# AND CARING

You yourselves are all the
endorsement we need. Your very
lives are a letter that anyone can
read by just looking at you.
Christ himself wrote it—
not with ink, but with God's
living Spirit; not chiseled into
stone, but carved into human
lives—and we publish it.

2 Corinthians 3:1–3, from *The Message*
— Eugene Peterson

# OUR MAJOR CONCERN

"Do not be deceived: God cannot be mocked. A man reaps what he sows. The one who sows to please his sinful nature, from that nature will reap destruction; the one who sows to please the Spirit, from the Spirit will reap eternal life. Let us not become weary in doing good, for at the proper time we will reap a harvest if we do not give up. Therefore, as we have opportunity, *let us do good to all people, especially to those who belong to the family of believers.*"

## Galatians 6:7–10

Having reached the conclusion that life's greatest purpose is to channel God's tender, loving care to others, the next question we must consider is this: In caring for others, is there to be any order or priority? Do we concern ourselves equally with Christians and non-Christians, or does one take precedence over the other? The Scripture, I believe, is quite clear on this matter. The Living Bible translates the text before us today thus: "We should always be kind to every one, and *especially* to our Christian brothers" (v. 10). While we must have a genuine concern for everyone, our major concern must be toward our fellow Christians.

## A Healthy Church

The view by many Christians (and which at one time I held myself) is this: we must minister to the unconverted first, as ailing Christians will make it to heaven—the unconverted will not. I have come to see that this is a very shortsighted view.

Why is it that the Christian church here in the West is unable to make much of an impression on the non-Christian community? There are many reasons, of course, but the major one is because the church is filled with weak, dispirited, and immature believers who fail to fully reflect the joy and love of Jesus Christ. If the church were healthy and mainly filled with mature Christians, then we would not need to be involved in so much aggressive evangelism. The non-Christian, seeing a joyous and loving church, would be drawn toward it by the sheer attractiveness of love. Lack of spiritual maturity in believers is a deterrent to others receiving the gospel. We must get things the right way around, and thus avoid the criticism made by many that the church is the only society that doesn't take care of its wounded.

O Father, I see that the depth of the church's outreach to the world is directly related to the depth of its maturity. Make me mature so I can show others the way. Amen.

Our major concern must be toward our fellow Christians.

# THE MAIN FOCUS

"However, if you suffer as a Christian, do not be ashamed, but praise God that you bear that name. *For it is time for judgment to begin with the family of God*; and if it begins with us, what will the outcome be for those who do not obey the gospel of God? And,

> 'If it is hard for the righteous to be saved,
> what will become of the ungodly and the sinner?'

So then, those who suffer according to God's will should commit themselves to their faithful Creator and continue to do good."

1 Peter 4:16–19

Some churches are so keen on evangelism that they overlook the fact that their primary responsibility is to build and develop a healthy Christian community. This latter responsibility should never be allowed to develop into an unhealthy introspection, of course. God forbid. Now don't misunderstand me, I am not against evangelism. I have been an evangelist for most of my Christian life and still engage from time to time in active evangelism. I love preaching the gospel to the unconverted; nevertheless, I have to say that my *major* concern is to see Christians come to maturity.

## Caring for God's Family

Let's face it—the Christian church is seriously lacking in

love, joy, and maturity. We show little care and concern for those in our midst who are weak and ailing. How can we say we care for sinners if we don't care for those who are part of the family of God? In some of our churches there is such a lack of concern for spiritual development and maturity that if a new Christian came in, he would be in danger of suffocating in such an atmosphere. Even the healthiest baby cannot thrive if left to fend for itself!

This, however, should not be taken to mean that we stop our evangelistic efforts until the church is where it should be. Reaching out to the unconverted must be very much in our minds but so, too, must the building up of the body of Christ. And the latter must have our main focus of concentration. Jesus did not say, "By this all men will know that you are my disciples, if you hold evangelistic rallies in the Royal Albert Hall or Wembley Stadium." No, He said, "By this all men will know that you are my disciples, if you have love for one another" (John 13:35 RSV). The world listens when Christians love.

O Father, You cut through our armored defenses with the sword of Your Spirit. But Your strokes save rather than sever, for You are love and only love. I, too, want to be love. For Jesus' sake. Amen.

The world listens when Christians love.

# CANNIBAL CHRISTIANS

"You, my brothers, were called to be free. But do not use your freedom to indulge the sinful nature; rather, serve one another in love. The entire law is summed up in a single command: 'Love your neighbor as yourself.' *If you keep on biting and devouring each other, watch out or you will be destroyed by each other.* So I say, live by the Spirit, and you will not gratify the desires of the sinful nature. For the sinful nature desires what is contrary to the Spirit, and the Spirit what is contrary to the sinful nature. They are in conflict with each other, so that you do not do what you want. But if you are led by the Spirit, you are not under law."

## Galatians 5:13–18

We have been emphasizing over the past few days that before the church can effectively communicate to the world that God loves people and cares for them. This caring love must itself be seen in the community life of the church. Unless it is, then all we have to offer is just something to say, rather than something to show. If all we have is something to say, then that tends to make people feel inferior. But if what we say is backed up by a certain kind of lifestyle, this makes the message singularly attractive. Although there are many churches where love and care are practiced by the members toward each other, there are far too many where it is not. In fact, many are nests of hate, where instead of love and care, there exists spite and spleen.

## Freedom?

Some years ago I stayed with a family whose child asked me if I knew where in the Bible it spoke about "cannibal Christians." I racked my brains and confessed I knew of no such Scripture. She pointed me to today's verse. The J. B. Phillips translation puts it thus: "But if freedom means merely that you are free to attack and tear one another to pieces, be careful that it doesn't mean that between you, you destroy your fellowship altogether!"

Are there any "cannibal Christians" in your church? If the sheep are not protected from the wolves, then it is to be expected that they will get bitten, but no shepherd would expect his sheep to get bitten in the barn! The tragedy in some of our churches is that often the greatest wounds come not from the wolves but from other sheep. Christians in such churches need to put on their "Ephesians 6 armor," not merely to protect themselves from the devil, but also to protect themselves from each other.

O Father, send the wind of Your caring love through every part of Your church so that the world might see and not just hear it proclaimed. For Jesus' sake. Amen.

Caring love must itself be seen in the community life of the church.

# ETHOS, PATHOS, AND LOGIA

"If I speak in the tongues of men and of angels, but have not love, I am only a resounding gong or a clanging cymbal. If I have the gift of prophecy and can fathom all mysteries and all knowledge, and *if I have a faith that can move mountains, but have not love, I am nothing.* If I give all I possess to the poor and surrender my body to the flames, but have not love, I gain nothing. Love is patient, love is kind. It does not envy, it does not boast, it is not proud. It is not rude, it is not self-seeking, it is not easily angered, it keeps no record of wrongs. Love does not delight in evil but rejoices with the truth. It always protects, always trusts, always hopes, always perseveres."

## 1 Corinthians 13:1–7

We continue emphasizing the need for the church to become a loving, caring community so that its message to the world might be presented with maximum effectiveness.

## Messengers

One of the terms used by communicators is the phrase, "the medium is the message." This means that it is impossible to separate a message from the manner in which it is given. The message is wrapped up in the messenger. Even the pagan Greeks understood this concept, for Aristotle said that

the proclaimer of any message had to have three things—
*ethos, pathos,* and *logia.* First, he must have *ethos,* which is
related to our word *ethical.* The finest communicator loses
his credibility if his integrity is in doubt. The second quality
is *pathos,* which means sympathy or empathy. People want
to know, when they listen to a message, if the messenger shares
their hopes, their fears, and their longings. The Greeks
recognized that oratorical skill without a caring heart added
up to nothing. "Eloquence without love," said the apostle,
"is a sounding brass and a tinkling cymbal." An American
evangelist, Floyd McClung, put it succinctly when he
said, "People don't care how much we know until they
know how much we care."

The third quality is *logia,* closely related to "logos"
or "word." The person who communicates must have
something to say. Non-Christians need a demonstration,
a visual aid that reveals the gospel as being good news.
*Ethos* and *pathos* are character qualities and can be seen:
they address themselves to the motives and needs of the
human heart. These, when evident, help prepare the non-
Christian community to listen to the words *(logia)* of the gospel.

O Father, save us from becoming self-centered and
uncaring, and from speaking so loudly that people
can't hear what we say. In Jesus' name. Amen.

The message is wrapped up in the messenger.

# STEREOPHONIC SAINTS

"Who is going to harm you if you are eager to do good? But even if you should suffer for what is right, you are blessed. 'Do not fear what they fear; do not be frightened.' *But in your hearts set apart Christ as Lord. Always be prepared to give an answer to everyone who asks you to give the reason for the hope that you have. But do this with gentleness and respect*, keeping a clear conscience, so that those who speak maliciously against your good behavior in Christ may be ashamed of their slander. It is better, if it is God's will, to suffer for doing good than for doing evil. For Christ died for sins once for all, the righteous for the unrighteous, to bring you to God."

1 Peter 3:13—18a

We ended yesterday by saying that *ethos* and *pathos* (integrity and empathy) help prepare the non-Christian community to hear the "words" (*logia*) of the gospel. It is my conviction that if this fact is not taken seriously by the contemporary Christian church, then the cause of world evangelism is ultimately futile. Unfortunately, most evangelistic courses focus on how to mouth the words of the gospel— not many focus on how to play the music. The lyrics, without the musical accompaniment, lose much of their impact. The Bible encourages us to use both in our communication with the world.

## Living the Life

In the text before us today, Peter says, "Quietly trust yourself to Christ your Lord and if anybody asks you why you believe as you do, be ready to tell him [words], and do it in a gentle and respectful way [music]." There are occasions when the music might be more effective than the words. Listen to what Peter says in the same chapter to wives with spiritually indifferent husbands: "Wives, fit in with your husbands' plans; for then if they refuse to listen when you talk to them about the Lord [words], they will be won by your respectful, pure behavior. Your godly lives [music] will speak to them better than any words" (vv. 1–2 TLB).

Evangelism is to be stereophonic. God speaks to His erring creatures through two channels: the written word (the Bible) and you—His "living epistle." The best argument for Christianity is Christians—their joy, their love, their care and concern. The church of today has the best lyrics but some very poor music. Let's begin to play the music, and then the world will be more ready to listen to the Word.

Gracious and loving Father, how tenderly
You put Your finger on our problems. Help us—
Your people—to be truly stereophonic,
sharing the love of Jesus both by our lips
and by our lives. Amen.

Sharing the love of Jesus both by our lips and by our lives.

# THE MUSIC OF
# THE GOSPEL

"You are the salt of the earth. But if the salt loses its saltiness, how can it be made salty again? It is no longer good for anything, except to be thrown out and trampled by men. You are the light of the world. A city on a hill cannot be hidden. Neither do people light a lamp and put it under a bowl. Instead they put it on its stand, and it gives light to everyone in the house. In the same way, let your light shine before men, *that they may see your good deeds and praise your Father in heaven.*"

## Matthew 5:13–16

We said yesterday that as far as the presentation of our message to the world is concerned, the lyrics need to be backed up by the music. Christians are to *be* good news before they *share* the good news. In today's church, we have evangelism the wrong way around. We say: "Here are the words; the music will come later." But evangelism would be far more effective if the music of the gospel preceded the words and thus prepared the hearts of the people for what is to follow.

## Words and Music

What is the *music* of the gospel? First, let me clarify the meaning of the word *gospel.* The gospel is the good news that Jesus Christ came to this earth to die for our sins and redeem us from death, hell, and destruction. The Living Bible puts it so well: "But God showed his great love for us by sending Christ to die for us while we were still sinners" (Rom. 5:8). That's the wonder of the gospel—that God broke into human history and made a way where there was no way.

As the gospel makes an impact on people's lives, and it works its way out through their relationships so that their lifestyle is transformed—then that becomes the music. When the world observes Christian couples loving each other, and both husbands and wives supporting and caring for their families, when they see churches overflowing with care and concern, they have seen a miracle—they have heard the music. It is the miraculous music for which so many people are longing. The two greatest forces in evangelism today are a caring family and a caring church. The two are inter-dependent. You can't have one without the other.

O Father, help me to be such a loving, caring person that even though I may stumble over my lines, the music will play on—mightily and miraculously. For Jesus' sake. Amen.

God broke into human history.

# Out Of Business

"To the angel of the church in Ephesus write: These are the words of him who holds the seven stars in his right hand and walks among the seven golden lampstands: I know your deeds, your hard work and your perseverance. I know that you cannot tolerate wicked men, that you have tested those who claim to be apostles but are not, and have found them false. You have persevered and have endured hardships for my name, and have not grown weary. Yet I hold this against you: You have forsaken your first love. Remember the height from which you have fallen! Repent and do the things you did at first. *If you do not repent, I will come to you and remove your lampstand from its place.*"

### Revelation 2:1–5

We said earlier that the world listens when Christians care. Consequently, the corporate image of the local church in its community is a critical factor in assessing its evangelistic impact. "In the final analysis," says James Engel, "the church is both message and medium, exemplifying and proclaiming the kingdom of God."

## Ambassadors or Embarrassment?

The church, unfortunately, has far too many Christians who recite the words but have little or no music. They fight, they gossip, they argue, they resist, they wrangle and they act, as someone said, "as if they were weaned on pickles."

Such Christians, instead of being ambassadors to the world, are an embarrassment to the world. The body of Christ, like a living organism, is prone to disease, and if the disease goes unchecked, the organism is greatly weakened. What a tragedy that the church, having so many opportunities for evangelism, is greatly weakened by this inner rot.

The theologically orthodox church at Ephesus was warned by God that if she did not recover her love, then He would remove her lampstand—put her out of business. God is saying the same thing to the churches of this generation: "Demonstrate love, or I will withdraw my presence." Can it be that many of the places where people meet on Sundays to sing a few hymns are churches in name only? Honesty compels us to admit that this may be so. If a church does not focus on conducting God's business—being a loving, caring community—then it must not complain if, in due course, it finds itself out of business!

Jesus, my Lord and Master, in the light of these sobering thoughts, I have but one request: You shared Your love with me; help me to catch the fire of Your sharing. My motto shall be: freely have I received, freely I give. Amen.

"Demonstrate love, or I will withdraw my presence."

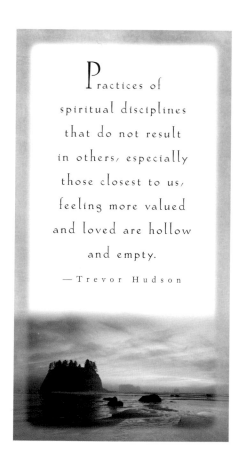

Practices of spiritual disciplines that do not result in others, especially those closest to us, feeling more valued and loved are hollow and empty.

— Trevor Hudson

*J o u r n a l    E n t r y*

_____

_____

_____

_____

_____

_____

_____

_____

_____

_____

_____

_____

_____

_____

_____

_____

_____

_____

_____

_____

_____

# WHO SHOULD WE LOVE BEST IN THIS LIFE?

Self-hatred is an indecent
luxury that no disciple can afford.
Self-hatred subtly reestablishes me
as the center of my focus and
concern. Biblically that is idolatry.
Gentleness toward myself issues
in gentleness with others.

— Brennan Manning

# S E L F - C E N T E R E D —
# S E L F - D I S R U P T E D

"We who are strong ought to bear with the failings of the weak and not to please ourselves. Each of us should please his neighbor for his good, to build him up. For even Christ did not please himself but, as it is written: 'The insults of those who insult you have fallen on me.' For everything that was written in the past was written to teach us, so that through endurance and the encouragement of the Scriptures we might have hope. May the God who gives endurance and encouragement give you a spirit of unity among yourselves as you follow Christ Jesus, so that with one heart and mouth you may glorify the God and Father of our Lord Jesus Christ."

## Romans 15:1—6

We turn now to consider another vital question in relation to the matter of caring: What happens if we fail to reach out and help others? The answer is that we become inextricably involved with ourselves and our own problems and troubles. The person who says, "I couldn't care less," has to care more—about himself. That is the payoff. Caring is, as we have seen, a basic law of life. Break it and you get broken—there are no exceptions.

## How to Become Unhappy

While browsing once in a bookstore, I came across a

book entitled *Care for Yourself Only.* I quickly skimmed it and discovered that its central theme was that it was one's duty and responsibility to care for oneself and ignore the needs of others. I asked the proprietor if anyone bought such a book, and he said that it was gaining a large following, especially among young people. I am not a prophet, but I predict that the followers of this idea will become a group of disillusioned, cynical, self-centered men and women, insistent on having their own way and then not liking their way after they get it. They will express themselves and then not like the self they express.

It can be said (and proved) that every self-centered person is an unhappy person—no exceptions. This matter of centering on oneself works badly—in fact, it works havoc on the very self which is being centered upon. Every self-centered person is a disrupted person, and the disruption doesn't stop with the soul or the spirit; it extends straight out into the nerves and tissues and poisons them with disease, functional and structural. More people are being broken by self-centeredness than any other thing in life.

O Father, help me to be a truly adjusted person—
adjusted to You and adjusted to life. I see that
I cannot center on myself without going to rack
and ruin. Release me from self-centeredness into
Christ-centeredness. For Jesus' sake. Amen.

Every self-centered person is an unhappy person.

# TO SAVE—IS TO LOSE

"But when Jesus turned and looked at his disciples, he rebuked Peter, 'Out of my sight, Satan!' he said. 'You do not have in mind the things of God, but the things of men.' Then he called the crowd to him along with his disciples and said: 'If anyone would come after me, he must deny himself and take up his cross and follow me. *For whoever wants to save his life will lose it*, but whoever loses his life for me and for the gospel will save it. What good is it for a man to gain the whole world, yet forfeit his soul? Or what can a man give in exchange for his soul?'"

## Mark 8:33–37

We ended yesterday by saying that more people are broken by self-centeredness than any other thing in life. The text before us today: "For whoever wants to save his life will lose it . . ." underlines the fact that when we concentrate on ourselves, the self will go to pieces, not only spiritually but, so I believe, mentally and physically as well.

## Egocentricity

A famous doctor said, "Every self-centered person draws disease to himself as a magnet draws iron filings to itself." He cited the case of a girl who was overprivileged. She had everything thrown into her lap—money, opportunity, a good education, prestige, and so on, but she was so self-centered that she could enjoy none of them. Every sickness that came into the neighborhood affected her. She drew illness toward her like a magnet. "That," said the doctor, "is the end of egocentrics. They start out to draw life to themselves— its joys, its thrills—and all they succeed in drawing to themselves is sadness, disillusionment, and sickness— spiritual, mental, and physical."

Someone gave me as a birthday present many years ago a book entitled *What Makes Sammy Run?* It had little spiritual content but it brought home to me, more than any other book I have read, the fact that egocentricity has its own punishment. The author, after tracing Sammy's egocentric but apparently successful life, sums up in these words: "Sammy got what was coming to him—not in a sudden payoff, but a process, a disease . . . the symptoms intensifying: success, loneliness, fear. I thought, 'You're alone, pal, all alone. That's the way you wanted it; that's the way you've got it.'" When we concentrate on ourselves alone, then the law of the universe goes into operation—we save our life, only to lose it.

O God, my Father, You have wrought Your laws into the very texture of my being. How foolish for me to run against those laws and imagine I can get away with it. I cannot get away from You. Help me to live for others—then I will truly live. Amen.

Help me to live for others—then I will truly live.

# PEOPLE PICKELED
# IN THEMSELVES

"One man considers one day more sacred than another; another man considers every day alike. Each one should be fully convinced in his own mind. He who regards one day as special, does so to the Lord. He who eats meat, eats to the Lord, for he gives thanks to God; and he who abstains, does so to the Lord and gives thanks to God. *For none of us lives to himself alone* and none of us dies to himself alone. If we live, we live to the Lord; and if we die, we die to the Lord. So, whether we live or die, we belong to the Lord."

Romans 14:5–8

We continue examining a very important principle of life—that when we reach out to others and care for them, we become less and less concerned about our own troubles and difficulties and less and less prone to personality problems. Dr. Karl Menninger, a famous psychiatrist, once said to a group of students: "If you come across someone who is on the verge of a nervous breakdown, then here is a sound piece of advice—get them to go across the tracks and do something positive for them. You may not always be successful in motivating them to do this, but if you can, and they participate in helping others then the threatened nervous breakdown will dissolve of its own accord."

## Giving One's Life

The mental health specialists are beginning to emphasize what the Bible has been emphasizing for centuries, that to save one's life, one has to give it. Those in psychiatric care are largely suffering from one thing in various forms—self-centered preoccupation. Some forms of mental illness are generated by physical factors, I know, but, generally speaking, the reason people become mentally ill is because, for one reason or another, they become immersed in themselves.

When a consultant psychiatrist was asked if his patients were beside themselves, he replied, "No, they are very much themselves. They have no interest beyond themselves. They are pickled in themselves: that's why they are here." However, many others, too, are tied up inwardly and are walking conflicts who never receive professional help. They stay in normal relationships, only to make them abnormal by their inner conflicts.

O Father, I must be released completely from the claims of self-interest and self-centeredness. May this week be a week not only of learning but of liberty. In Christ's name I pray. Amen.

Reaching out to others and caring for them.

# THE PURPOSE OF THE ATONEMENT

"For Christ's love compels us, because we are convinced that one died for all, and therefore all died. And *he died for all, that those who live should no longer live for themselves* but for him who died for them and was raised again. So from now on we regard no one from a worldly point of view. Though we once regarded Christ in this way, we do so no longer. Therefore, if anyone is in Christ, he is a new creation; the old has gone, the new has come! All this is from God, who reconciled us to himself through Christ and gave us the ministry of reconciliation: that God was reconciling the world to himself in Christ, not counting men's sins against them. And he has committed to us the message of reconciliation."

2 Corinthians 5:14–19

We are quietly coming to the conclusion that we were created by God to be caring and concerned people, and when we abandon this divine design for one of self-interest, we live against life's greatest purpose and end up with inner conflicts and self-disruption. When the director of a large psychiatric hospital was asked how so few nurses could control so many people—wouldn't they organize themselves and break out?—he replied, "No, the seriously mentally ill never organize." They were made for outgoing love, made for cooperation and creative activity, but now, because of inner pain and external pressure, they had retreated into self-interest, thus ending up in inner conflict and disorganization.

## Freeing Power

A newspaper report I read once told of a minister visiting a home for the care of the mentally ill, and, knowing the people there had a good deal of spare time on their hands, he invited them to participate in a scheme to help the victims of a local flood disaster. He expected a rush of people after his talk ended, eager and ready to offer their services. Not one person came forward. He said, "I then realized why they were there; they were bounded by their own problems and hence bound by them."

Our text for today spells out the good news that one of the chief ends of Christ's atonement is to deliver us from self-centered preoccupation. Have you experienced the freeing power of the cross in relation to this matter of your self-centeredness? Some people experience it in a dramatic moment of conversion. Most, however, find it some time after conversion in a period of enlightenment and challenge such as God is taking us through this week.

O Father, I am so thankful that Your atonement did not pass by my central need—the need of deliverance from myself. May this be a week of emancipation and spiritual release. For Jesus' sake.

My central need—deliverance from myself.

# S E L F — S U R R E N D E R

"You foolish Galatians! Who has bewitched you? Before your very eyes Jesus Christ was clearly portrayed as crucified. I would like to learn just one thing from you: Did you receive the Spirit by observing the law, or by believing what you heard? Are you so foolish? *After beginning with the Spirit, are you now trying to attain your goal by human effort?* Have you suffered so much for nothing—if it really was for nothing? Does God give you his Spirit and work miracles among you because you observe the law, or because you believe what you heard? Consider Abraham: 'He believed God, and it was credited to him as righteousness.'"

## Galatians 3:1–6

We are meditating on the need for a full and complete deliverance from self. Today we examine the three most popular views of the self held by theorists. They are as follows: *know yourself, accept yourself,* and *express yourself.* All three are valid concepts, providing they are linked with Christ and not divorced from Him.

## Yourself and God

Take the first concept—know yourself. How can you know yourself unless you know God? You are a child of God, made in His likeness, and so it follows that you can only know yourself as you know Him.

The second affirmation is *accept yourself.* Outside of God and Christ, how is it possible for a person to really accept himself? If he accepts himself on the level of an unredeemed sinner, then he himself is unacceptable to himself. A man who was accepted by a club which had very high entrance standards said, as soon as he heard he was now a member: "I resign: I can no longer belong to a club that would have a man like me as a member." Only when a person has been changed by Christ is he truly able to accept himself.

The third affirmation of present-day thinkers is *express yourself.* However, here again, outside of Christ, what kind of self can a person express? Only an egocentric self, a proud self, a sinful self. The advice of the non-Christian social scientists is to put self in the center; but this is diametrically opposite to the Bible's teaching. Anything that leaves you at the center is off-center. It feeds the disease it is trying to cure, namely, self-centeredness. The secular way lacks the vital principle that only the Christian faith offers—self-surrender.

My Father and my God, I realize I am on the verge of discovering one of life's greatest secrets—deliverance from self. Hold me fast so that over the next two days I might come to a full and complete deliverance. Amen.

You can only know yourself as you know Him.

# A WILLING CRUCIFIXION

"If, while we seek to be justified in Christ, it becomes evident that we ourselves are sinners, does that mean that Christ promotes sin? Absolutely not! If I rebuild what I destroyed, I prove that I am a lawbreaker. For through the law I died to the law so that I might live for God. *I have been crucified with Christ and I no longer live, but Christ lives in me.* The life I live in the body, I live by faith in the Son of God, who loved me and gave himself for me. I do not set aside the grace of God, for if righteousness could be gained through the law, Christ died for nothing!"

## Galatians 2:17–21

We are seeing that none of the secular approaches to the problem of the self are adequate or effective. Self-knowledge, self-acceptance, self-expression—all valid concepts in themselves—must be preceded by self-surrender if a person is to live effectively on this earth.

## Surrendering

The question now arises: How do we go about the task of surrendering ourselves to God? You may have already experienced a partial surrendering of yourself, but now it is time for a *full* surrender. Paul shows us the way: "I have been crucified with Christ and I no longer live, but Christ lives in me." What an amazing truth: the "I" is crucified—and yet alive. How can this be? The principle of self-surrender is this: the self, or ego, is offered up *lovingly* as Jesus offered Himself up on the cross. Christ's offering was done out of love. Our offering of ourselves to be crucified with Him must also be out of love. We love Him so much that we can withhold nothing from Him—not even our very self. We must *willingly* consent to be crucified with Christ, for the unwilling crucifixion has no resurrection in it—it is death and only death. However, when we willingly consent to be crucified with Christ, we die with Him and rise with Him.

An inscription I saw on a letter I received recently, which gave rise to the thoughts I am expressing today, said, "He who is nailed to the cross willingly—walks the earth free." What profundity! After being crucified with Christ, Paul was more alive than ever—alive to his fingertips: "Christ lives in me." Christ, who is life, was living in him!

O Father, I see that if I do not consent to be crucified with Christ, then I unwillingly crucify myself through my own conflicts and contradictions. Today I willingly offer myself to You: that self might die and Christ might live in me, heightening all my powers. Amen.

Today I willingly offer myself to you.

# GAZING AT
# SUFFERING LOVE

*"Your attitude should be the same as that of Christ Jesus:*

Who, being in very nature God,
>        did not consider equality with God something
>        to be grasped,
but made himself nothing,
>        taking the very nature of a servant,
>        being made in human likeness.
And being found in appearance as a man,
>        he humbled himself
>        and became obedient to death—
>        even death on a cross!
Therefore God exalted him to the highest place
>        and gave him the name that is above every name,
>        that at the name of Jesus every knee should bow,
>        in heaven and on earth and under the earth,
and every tongue confess that Jesus Christ is Lord,
>        to the glory of God the Father."

## Philippians 2:5—11

We must spend one more day discussing the important matter of self-surrender. If the center of the word *sin* is I, then the center of the deliverance from sin is the deliverance from the "I." We are not fully Christian until we know how to surrender the self.

## A Possibility and a Power

Someone said once in a letter to me: "Isn't the whole business of redemption concerned with getting us into heaven?" I replied: "No, that is perhaps the final purpose. But the one great purpose God has for us here on earth is to get heaven into us." You can't really live with "heaven" inside you until the self has been properly put in its place—into the hands of Christ. Your self in your own hands is a problem—your self in the hands of Christ is a possibility and a power. Look hard and long at the cross today, for the surest way to break down any resistance you may have to self-surrender is to gaze at Christ's suffering love.

A teenage girl was told that if she stayed out late she would get bread and water for supper. She stayed out late, and at supper time she was given bread and water as promised. After a few minutes her father reached over and took the bread and water, giving his daughter his own meal instead. Something broke inside her. Self-will was broken and "father-will" was gently substituted by her own choice. No threat of punishment, no fear of consequences could work that miracle. Only suffering love could do that. So stand before the cross and gaze upward into that loving face. See how suffering love has taken your punishment and pain. Lift your ego to Him for cleansing and redirection, and walk away from the cross, free from self-interest and self-concern.

Lord, I accept, right now, Your full and complete deliverance. Delivered from myself, I am now free to give myself to others. Amen.

Look long and hard at the cross today.

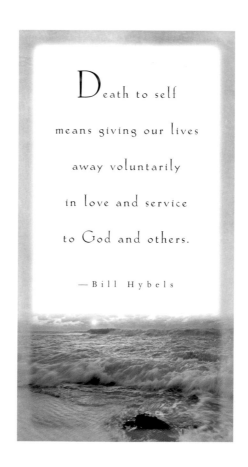

Death to self means giving our lives away voluntarily in love and service to God and others.

—Bill Hybels

# Journal Entry

_____

_____

_____

_____

_____

_____

_____

_____

_____

_____

_____

_____

_____

_____

_____

_____

_____

_____

_____

# WHAT IS CHRISTIAN CARING?

Listening is the 'highest form of hospitality.' There we do not set out 'to change people but to offer them space where change can take place.'

— Henri Nouwen

# CARING
# IS COMMITMENT

"Now listen, you who say, 'Today or tomorrow we will go to this or that city, spend a year there, carry on business and make money.' Why, you do not even know what will happen tomorrow. What is your life? You are a mist that appears for a little while and then vanishes. Instead, you ought to say, 'If it is the Lord's will, we will live and do this or that.' As it is, you boast and brag. All such boasting is evil. *Anyone, then, who knows the good he ought to do and doesn't do it, sins.*"

James 4:13–17

What exactly is Christian caring? This is the question that will occupy our thoughts and attention over the coming week. Caring is attending to the welfare of other people, reaching out to them in ways that help them see and understand the character of Christ as manifested through our deeds, our words, and our actions. Caring is more than liking a person, comforting a person, or showing sympathy to a person. Caring is a commitment, an action of the will which is dedicated to obeying another deep law of the universe—*it is more blessed to give than to receive.*

## Giving

Some time ago I heard of a lady who attended a church

where the minister and the elders laid great emphasis on giving—the giving of one's time, tithes, and talents to the Lord. One Sunday morning after an especially strong appeal, she approached the minister and said, "All you seem to think about in this church is give, give, give." "My dear," said the minister gently, "I must thank you for supplying me with one of the best definitions of the Christian life."

It is important to recognize that caring is more than a feeling, more than a mood, more than an emotion. It is an attitude of mind that applies itself to doing what God expects of us, whether we feel like it or not. The Epistle of James says: "Anyone, then, who knows the good he ought to do and doesn't do it, sins." When we know the right thing to do, even though we may not feel like doing it, then not doing it is, according to Scripture, a sin. This is not to say that feeling is not involved, but if you wait for feelings, they may arrive too late. Caring is commitment—the actions are taken, whether feeling is there or not.

O God, give me clear insight and courage
to lay hold on this truth, for it challenges me to
the very depth of my being. Help me not to be
guided by my feelings but by a dedicated will.
In Jesus' name I pray. Amen.

It is more blessed to give than to receive.

# C A R I N G

# I s  L i s t e n i n g

"My dear brothers, take note of this: *Everyone should be quick to listen*, slow to speak and slow to become angry, for man's anger does not bring about the righteous life that God desires. Therefore, get rid of all moral filth and the evil that is so prevalent, and humbly accept the word planted in you, which can save you. Do not merely listen to the word, and so deceive yourselves. Do what it says."

James 1:19–22

We continue meditating on the question: What is caring? We said yesterday that caring is a commitment of the will to do what Christ expects of us—whether we feel like it or not. With that thought in mind, let us try to think through together what caring means in real and practical terms.

## Concentrated Listening

One of the most caring things we can do for people is to *listen* to them. Listening means concentrating on what another person is saying so intently that you become more aware of the other person than you are of yourself. It's not easy to listen like that, as society teaches us to express ourselves rather than to listen. Listening is an art. It begins with the way we use our eyes. When people talk to you, they receive lots of messages about how interested you are in them by the way your body talks. If you look beyond persons instead of at them, the message they receive is that you are not all that deeply interested in what they are saying. Dr. Julias Fast says, "If you hold another person's eye longer than say two seconds, it's a clear sign to them that you are interested in what they are saying." Don't overdo this and spend the rest of the day staring into people's eyes, because obviously this principle can be taken too far. But ask the Lord to help you become a good listener and to listen to others as He listens to you.

One man I know, an expert in the art of listening, told me that occasionally, when he listens to people sharing problems or unveiling their deepest feelings, he notices a moistness gathering around their eyes, as if to say, "Thank God! At last I'm being heard!"

> O Father, I am humbled by the thought
> that whenever I talk to You, not once have
> You turned away from me and not listened.
> If caring means listening, then make me
> a good listener. For Jesus' sake. Amen.

Listening is an art.

# CARING
# IS TOUCHING

"A man with leprosy came and knelt before him and said, 'Lord, if you are willing, you can make me clean.' *Jesus reached out his hand and touched the man.* 'I am willing,' he said. 'Be clean!' Immediately he was cured of his leprosy. Then Jesus said to him, 'See that you don't tell anyone. But go, show yourself to the priest and offer the gift Moses commanded, as a testimony to them.'"

## Matthew 8:2—4

After saying yesterday that caring is listening, we now consider another important principle of caring—*caring is touching*. A minister tells of visiting a children's ward in a hospital where a young doctor was reported to be greatly loved by the children. Whenever he walked into the ward, they received him with delight and joy. His colleagues couldn't understand why, and so one night they secretly watched him as he made his evening round. Then the mystery was solved. He touched every child gently on the face as he said goodnight.

## The Power of Touch

Ashley Montagu has written a long and scholarly book on the art of touching. He says the skin is the most sensitive organ of our body. A human being can survive blindness, deafness, or even loss of the senses of smell and taste, but it is impossible to survive, he says, without the function of the skin. During the nineteenth century a high percentage of infants in orphanages died from a disease called *marasmus*. A distinguished pediatrician, Dr. Chapin, noted that infants were rarely picked up or touched, so he brought in women to hold the babies, coo to them, and stroke them. The mortality rate dropped drastically.

If you want to demonstrate to others that you care, be aware of the power you have in your hands. But here again, don't overdo it. Physical gushing is as offensive as verbal gushing. When someone is hurting, reach out to them, put a hand gently on theirs or touch them gently on the shoulder. But, I say again, it must be done discreetly, tenderly, *and only for a moment*. When done as a genuine attempt to show you care, it can bring you closer to a person than a thousand words.

Lord, make me a person with a tender touch, and show me how to use, and not abuse, this means of communication. For Your own name's sake. Amen.

When people are hurting, reach out to them.

# CARING

# IS EMPATHY

"Praise be to the God and Father of our Lord Jesus Christ, the Father of compassion and the God of all comfort, *who comforts us in all our troubles, so that we can comfort those in any trouble* with the comfort we ourselves have received from God. For just as the sufferings of Christ flow over into our lives, so also through Christ our comfort overflows. If we are distressed, it is for your comfort and salvation; if we are comforted, it is for your comfort, which produces in you patient endurance of the same sufferings we suffer. And our hope for you is firm, because we know that just as you share in our sufferings, so also you share in our comfort."

## 2 Corinthians 1:3–7

Another principle of caring is *putting yourself in another person's place.* The imaginative ability to project yourself into another person's position is the key to life, for, as we said earlier, "life is sensitivity." I like the way someone defined empathy: "Your pain in my heart." Sometimes people say to me, "I'm not a very sympathetic person so this disqualifies me from the sympathetic role." I usually respond by saying, *"No, it doesn't, for sympathy can be learned."*

## Sympathy and Empathy

Let me pause here to clarify the difference between the

74

two words *sympathy* and *empathy*. Sympathy is subjective: it gets down into the pit with a person and shares his feelings of hurt. Empathy is objective: it seeks to understand the hurt, without going down into the pit, so that it can lift the other person to safety and security. This is why I prefer to use the word *empathy*—it is a more objective and more appropriate word in the present context.

Christians who are not empathic by nature can develop the mind-set of empathy. It involves a continuous, active effort to understand what is going on inside the other person's heart. Ask yourself questions like these: How would I feel if I were in this person's circumstances? How would I react if this had happened to me? If you are a person who is oversympathetic—that is, too subjective and you become overwhelmed by people's problems, then ask God to heal you of your inner hurts. Your overly sympathetic nature results from your own inner hurts which have never been healed, and are highlighted whenever you come in contact with someone who is hurting deeply.

Gracious Father, help me to become a truly empathic person—one who can feel for others without being swamped by those feelings. If I need inner healing, then heal me now. For Jesus' sake. Amen.

Sympathy can be *learned*.

# CARING

# IS RESPECT

"Love must be sincere. Hate what is evil; cling to what is good. *Be devoted to one another in brotherly love.* Honor one another above yourselves. Never be lacking in zeal, but keep your spiritual fervor, serving the Lord. Be joyful in hope, patient in affliction, faithful in prayer. Share with God's people who are in need. Practice hospitality. Bless those who persecute you; bless and do not curse. Rejoice with those who rejoice; mourn with those who mourn. Live in harmony with one another. Do not be proud, but be willing to associate with people of low position. Do not be conceited."

Romans 12:9–16

A fourth principle of caring is this: *caring is showing respect.* Some years ago a research project was conducted in the United States among a group of well-known psychiatrists and counselors to discover what qualities made them successful therapists. The researchers found one common denominator—the professionals had the ability to treat each of their counselees with profound respect. They did not belittle them or approach them in a superior attitude but came alongside them with the attitude, "I know you are hurting . . . I could have been in the same predicament . . . let me help you back on your feet."

## Caring Relationships

Unless we are careful, whenever we are confronted by people in need, we can adopt the attitude, "Isn't it wonderful that I am going to help you!" or, "How on earth did you allow yourself to get into such a mess? I would never have done such a thing." Caring avoids such attitudes. This, as I have said before, was one of the secrets of our Lord's success in His caring relationship with people: He differentiated between the sin and the sinner. He loathed people's sins, but He loved *them*. When you can do that—differentiate between people's problems and the person—then you are on your way to success in your role as a caring member of Christ's body.

Respect means that we care for people too much to judge them, categorize them, label them, or manipulate them. Instead, we will spend time showing love, concern, and a willingness to bear their burdens, and so fulfilling the law of Christ. Is it any wonder that Jesus was called "the friend of sinners"?

O Father, remove from my heart any attitude of superiority that may be there, and help me to relate to people with love, care, and respect. For Jesus' sake. Amen.

Differentiate between the sin and the sinner.

# CARING IS HOPE

*"Ask and it will be given to you;* seek and you will find; knock and the door will be opened to you. For everyone who asks receives; he who seeks finds; and to him who knocks, the door will be opened. Which of you, if his son asks for bread, will give him a stone? Or if he asks for a fish, will give him a snake? If you, then, though you are evil, know how to give good gifts to your children, how much more will your Father in heaven give good gifts to those who ask him! In everything, do to others what you would have them do to you, for this sums up the Law and the Prophets."

## Matthew 7:7–12

In our examination of the principles of caring, we come today to an extremely important one: *caring is giving hope.* Can you imagine how difficult it would be to care for someone if you couldn't offer hope? That's why I feel sorry for non-Christian psychiatrists and counselors who, despite their sincerest efforts, are unable to offer the hope that flows from Christ. There is, of course, natural hope, based on human reasoning and understanding. A person who is seriously ill, for example, can be greatly helped by a doctor who assures him or her that there is documented evidence to show that other people have recovered from this illness. This knowledge can create in the person a hope that is psychologically therapeutic.

## God Provides Help

The hope that I am referring to, however, is a Christian hope—the hope based on God's Word and character, the hope that in every trial and difficulty help will come from God. Has He not promised that when we ask, we shall receive; when we knock, it shall be opened; when we seek, we shall find? Learn to share this message with those who are hurting, and remind them that God is swift to come to the aid of those who are burdened, either to deliver them from their troubles or provide the grace that will enable them to transform their pain into a pearl.

The Christian hope does not encourage people to deny reality, or slip into inactivity, or engage in wishful thinking. It is hope that rests on the fact that God is all-wise, all-knowing and all-compassionate. However, such a truth is not easy to grasp when a person is under pressure. That is why God wants us to remind each other of it, especially in times of trouble.

Lord Jesus, make me a messenger of this truth to someone this very day. Help me to come alongside a wounded person and whisper that Jesus cares. For Your own dear name's sake. Amen.

God is all-wise, all-knowing, and all-compassionate.

# CARING IS UNDERSTANDING

"Be completely humble and gentle; *be patient, bearing with one another in love.* Make every effort to keep the unity of the Spirit through the bond of peace. There is one body and one Spirit—just as you were called to one hope when you were called—one Lord, one faith, one baptism; one God and Father of all, who is over all and through all and in all. But to each one of us grace has been given as Christ apportioned it."

## Ephesians 4:2–7

The final important principle in the caring relationship that we shall consider is: *caring is helping a person feel understood.* Everyone likes to feel understood, but how do we get across to people who are hurting that we understand them and their problem? We do it by reflecting to the person, in a paraphrased form, a summary of the problem as we see it. I emphasize the word *paraphrase* because there is nothing more inane and pointless than to repeat people's statements back to them verbatim.

## How to Offer Reassurance

I once overheard a Christian trying to help another who was obviously upset about something, and the conversation went something like this:

"I am feeling very upset with him."

"Hmm, I see, you are feeling upset with him."

"Yes, he had no right to talk to me like that."

"Hmm, he had no right to talk to you like that." "Yes, and what is more, I'm going to let him know how I feel."

"Hmm, you are going to let him know how you feel."

I could well imagine that person responding to the statement:

"I'm going to throw myself out of the window," in the same senseless manner, "Hmm, I see, you're going to throw yourself out of the window."

If you want to help people, then don't repeat exactly what they say. They will think they are talking to a parrot. Summarize it and phrase it in different words. This shows the person that you have grasped and comprehended the problem and gives him or her the reassurance that, even though you might not have a solution to the problem, at least you understand. And being understood is as helpful to the emotions as good advice is to the mind.

Father, help me to be skilful at this task
of helping people feel understood. Give me
opportunities to put it into practice this very day.
I am Yours—to use. Thank You, Father. Amen.

Being understood is helpful to the emotions.

Respect and genuineness are part of empathy. It means not 'to feel like' (that is sympathy) but 'to feel with.' It is about seeing the world through the other person's eyes, being accurately aware of her feelings and attempting to put them into words.

—Anne Long

_____

_____

_____

_____

_____

_____

_____

_____

_____

_____

_____

_____

_____

_____

_____

_____

_____

_____

_____

_____

_____

_____

# WEEK 5

## COMMON CHRISTIAN PROBLEMS

Love is the power behind the
hope that does not disappoint us.
Hope looks to the promise of the
final victory of Jesus Christ over
all that hurts and kills. When
a person knows he is loved he
has hope. Perhaps through the
touch of human care someone may
discover anew the saving love
of Christ, the Lord treating
him as a precious person.

— Lewis Smedes

# DOUBT

"Now that same day two of them were going to a village called Emmaus, about seven miles from Jerusalem. They were talking with each other about everything that had happened. As they talked and discussed these things with each other, Jesus himself came up and walked along with them; but they were kept from recognizing him. He asked them, 'What are you discussing together as you walk along?' They stood still, their faces downcast. One of them, named Cleopas, asked him, 'Are you the only one living in Jerusalem, who doesn't know the things that have happened there in these days?' 'What things?' he asked. 'About Jesus of Nazareth,' they replied. 'He was a prophet, powerful in word and deed before God and all the people.'"

## Luke 24:13–19

We turn now to focus on some of the more common problems and difficulties that arise from time to time in the hearts and minds of our fellow Christians. If we can know a little more about these problems, it will help us to develop a ministry of caring.

## Growing Through Grappling

One of the most common problems people struggle with is *doubt*. They doubt such things as whether God loves them, whether He answers prayer, and whether the Bible is true. How do we care for those in doubt? We must not allow ourselves to be upset when we come across fellow Christians who are struggling with doubt. As Os Guinness shows in his excellent book *In Two Minds*, going through the process of doubt can actually strengthen our faith. God may be allowing the person to wrestle with these doubts, for through grappling we grow. What you should not do is to say such things as, "Stop doubting," or, "Pull yourself together." That rarely helps. It is far more helpful to listen with compassion, acceptance, and love, although in listening you may hear things that distress you.

Keep in mind, as you listen, that most people's doubts are not in the mind but in the heart. Some doubts are intellectual, but most are emotional. By that I mean the person may be carrying a deep hurt which causes him or her to question the truth and reality of his or her intellectual beliefs. Don't be in too much of a hurry to give answers. Get alongside the person and show, by listening and understanding, that you care. Isn't this what Jesus did with the two believers on the way to Emmaus? He saw their doubt, and He could have dismissed it with the words: "I am the Lord." However, He waited, listened, and showed He cared. Then when He knew they were ready for revelation, He gave it.

Blessed Lord Jesus, teach me to get alongside people and not just confront them. Drive this truth deep into my spirit—that I must love people before I start giving them answers. Amen.

He waited, listened, and showed He cared.

# WHY SUFFERING?

"There are many parts, but one body. The eye cannot say to the hand, 'I don't need you!' And the head cannot say to the feet, 'I don't need you!' On the contrary, those parts of the body that seem to be weaker are indispensable, and the parts that we think are less honorable we treat with special honor. And the parts that are unpresentable are treated with special modesty, while our presentable parts need no special treatment. But God has combined the members of the body and has given greater honor to the parts that lacked it, so that there should be no division in the body, but that its parts should have equal concern for each other. *If one part suffers, every part suffers with it*; if one part is honored, every part rejoices with it."

## 1 Corinthians 12:20–26

Today we examine another common problem that arises from time to time in the hearts of fellow Christians. It is the problem of *suffering and pain.* It is often presented in this form: "Why does God allow me to suffer like this?" or, "Why doesn't He intervene to relieve me of my pain?"

## Sitting Alongside

For centuries Christians have struggled with the problem of suffering—and there are no easy answers. How do we care for people who are suffering and in pain? We do it by demonstrating that we are willing to take a little bit of their suffering and pain into ourselves. By that I mean that we encourage them to talk out their fears, their anxieties, their anger, even allowing it to fall upon ourselves. It's not easy to sit alongside someone who is suffering and allow him or her to unload fears or resentment into your heart. But this, I believe, is what Paul meant when he said, "Bear one another's burdens, and so fulfil the law of Christ" (Gal. 6:2 RSV).

We have already seen that the law of Christ is the law of caring. How much does Jesus care? He cared enough to hang on a cross and become, if you will pardon the expression, the "dumping ground" for our rebellion, anger, hatred, and distrust. In a lesser sense, He calls upon you and me to do the same. Do you care enough to sit alongside a person and become the "dumping ground" for his or her resentments, fears, and concerns? Don't worry if you don't have a good theological explanation for the problem of human suffering— just show the person that you care. You will pray, of course—pray for healing and release—but before you pray be willing to take a little of their pain into your own heart. Remember: "People don't care how much you know, but they do want to know how much you care."

O God, the thought of being a dumping ground for another's pain and suffering is foreign to my human nature. Deepen my compassion and my sensitivity to people so that I might truly be a caring person. For Jesus' sake. Amen.

People want to know how much you care.

# MEETING DISCOURAGEMENT

"By the meekness and gentleness of Christ, I appeal to you—I, Paul, who am 'timid' when face to face with you, but 'bold' when away! I beg you that when I come I may not have to be as bold as I expect to be toward some people who think that we live by the standards of this world. For though we live in the world, we do not wage war as the world does. The weapons we fight with are not the weapons of the world. On the contrary, they have divine power to demolish strongholds. We demolish arguments and every pretension that sets itself up against the knowledge of God, and *we take captive every thought to make it obedient to Christ.*"

## 2 Corinthians 10:1–5

Another common problem with which fellow Christians grapple *is the problem of discouragement*. It surfaces in statements such as this: "What's the use of trying?" "I give up," or, "Things are hopeless." In a world such as this, it is easy to become discouraged. How do we care for our brothers and sisters when they are overtaken by this problem? Here again, we meet it sensitively, lovingly, and with compassion. We listen, we understand, and we show our concern.

## Physical Causes

A great amount of research has been done in recent years on the subject of discouragement, and we have learned that sometimes discouragement can have physical causes. If a person is discouraged over a considerable period of time, it could be due to such things as poor sleeping habits, a chemical imbalance, physical infection, or improper diet. Obviously, you will pray with such a person, but if, after prayer, there is no dramatic change, encourage him or her to have a medical checkup. If no physical causes are found, help can be given by showing a person how to change his or her thinking.

Have you ever noticed how our emotions are affected by our thinking? It is impossible, by an act of will, to stop feeling discouraged, but if we work to change our thinking, then the feelings of discouragement often dissolve. Try to find out what the person is thinking, then very gently ask these questions: Is that thought really accurate? Is there proof of it? Is the situation being interpreted correctly? Could there be some other explanation? Discouraged people need, more than anything else, to get a new perspective on life. This can often come from a caring friend who lovingly dares to challenge and help change the discouraged person's thinking and conclusions.

Gracious Father, I am thankful for those who have come into my life with a kindly word and deep insight. Help me to be an agent of Your mind to some other person. For Your own name's sake. Amen.

Discouraged people need to get a new perspective on life.

# THE TYRANNY OF THE URGENT

"Now a man named Lazarus was sick. He was from Bethany, the village of Mary and her sister Martha. This Mary, whose brother Lazarus now lay sick, was the same one who poured perfume on the Lord and wiped his feet with her hair. So the sisters sent word to Jesus, 'Lord, the one you love is sick.' When he heard this, Jesus said, 'This sickness will not end in death. No, it is for God's glory so that God's Son may be glorified through it.' Jesus loved Martha and her sister and Lazarus. *Yet when he heard that Lazarus was sick, he stayed where he was two more days.*"

## John 11:1–6

We continue examining some of the more common problems that arise from time to time in the lives of fellow Christians. Today we look at the problem of *pressure and stress*. Work, housekeeping, looking after children, study, things that must be done at church, and a host of other demands build up a good deal of pressure. How do we care for people who are under pressure? Well, by now I hope it is quite clear that all problems should be met by good listening, by understanding, and by compassion. Having said that, let me go right to the heart of the problem.

## Important or Urgent

Pressure and stress arise from what someone has called "the tyranny of the urgent." This is a term used to describe the common habit of always doing what is most pressing instead of never taking the time to work out a proper order of priorities. One of the greatest mistakes people make is letting the urgent crowd out the important. The death of Lazarus illustrates this principle. What could have been more important than the urgent message from Mary and Martha, "Lord, the one you love is sick" (John 11:3)? Jesus' response to that was to stay where He was for two days. What was the urgent need? Obviously, to prevent the death of Lazarus. However, what was the important issue? To raise Lazarus from the dead. Jesus was able to recognize the difference between the urgent and the important.

If you see that fellow believers are under pressure, sit down with them and help them reevaluate their priorities. Make a list of activities in order of importance. Some things will have to go in the interests of health and good functioning. One of the most meaningful ways in which you can experience the delights of caring is to help people recognize the harmful effects of excessive pressure and assist them in building proper priorities.

Lord Jesus, You who so obviously lived a life free from the tyranny of the urgent, teach me how to build proper priorities so that I, in turn, might teach this principle to others. Amen.

Build proper priorities.

# OVERCOMING

# LOSS

"No discipline seems pleasant at the time, but painful. Later on, however, it produces a harvest of righteousness and peace for those who have been trained by it. Therefore, strengthen your feeble arms and weak knees. 'Make level paths for your feet,' so that the lame may not be disabled, but rather healed. Make every effort to live in peace with all men and to be holy; without holiness no one will see the Lord. *See to it that no one misses the grace of God* and that no bitter root grows up to cause trouble and defile many."

### Hebrews 12:11–15

If we are to undertake a caring ministry, another problem we ought to know something about is the problem of *loss*. No doubt someone in your church or fellowship is facing such a problem at this moment.

Loss comes in many ways—a child leaving home for college, a breakup of a romance, death of a loved one, redundancy, a separation or divorce. Each of these situations can bring a sense of grief. Each stirs up feelings of emptiness, loneliness, and a sense of bewilderment. How do we care for people who are feeling an acute sense of loss? Let me share with you a few principles that I have found useful in my own ministry when seeking to help a person face loss.

## Principles

*1. Help them to admit that they feel a sense of loss.* People can never overcome a problem until they admit they have one.

*2. Show them that it is not a weakness to lean on others at such a time.* Some people feel guilty about receiving help from others. Assure them that your care for them is given not grudgingly but joyously.

*3. Encourage them not to make any major decisions at the moment.* Some people rebound at times of loss and try to compensate for the sense of loss by rushing prematurely into new commitments.

*4. Help them see the need for a lot of rest, a regular schedule, and a proper diet.* This may not sound like deep "spiritual" advice but, believe me, it is.

*5. Make yourself available (daily if possible) so that the person can talk with you, pray with you, and share thoughts from the Scriptures.* In every church there are people facing loss, and this is better handled when there are people around like you who—although they may not have many answers—make it evident that they love and care.

O Father, the more I realize how many of my brothers and sisters are hurting, the more I feel constrained to care. Deepen my compassion and concern for people more and more. For Jesus' sake. Amen.

Make it evident that you love and care.

# STOP WORRYING

"Rejoice in the Lord always. I will say it again: Rejoice! Let your gentleness be evident to all. The Lord is near. *Do not be anxious about anything, but in everything, by prayer and petition, with thanksgiving, present your requests to God.* And the peace of God, which transcends all understanding, will guard your hearts and your minds in Christ Jesus. Finally, brothers, whatever is true, whatever is noble, whatever is right, whatever is pure, whatever is lovely, whatever is admirable—if anything is excellent or praiseworthy—think about such things. Whatever you have learned or received or heard from me, or seen in me—put it into practice. And the God of peace will be with you."

## Philippians 4:4–9

From time to time a common condition that arises in people's hearts is *worry and anxiety*. How do we care for those who are worried and anxious? Anxiety is a feeling of being threatened, apprehensive, and uneasy. Worry is the troublesome feeling we get when we become greatly concerned about real or imagined problems. The feelings of anxiety do not appear to spring from any reasonable cause. We can be anxious without knowing what exactly we are anxious about. Worry, on the other hand, has a traceable cause. When we worry, we usually know exactly what we are worrying about.

## Pray About Everything

A good biblical model for dealing with worry is found in the text before us today—a model we can use when dealing with those who are anxious and worried. We are told not to worry. That advice, coming from someone else, might not go down very well, but coming from God, it has point and purpose. To stop worrying is not to let our minds go blank. That will only last for a while, and then the worry will come back. God's method is to replace the worry by prayer: "Instead, pray about everything."

Sometimes, when dealing with worriers, I ask them to carry a card in their pocket with the words STOP WORRYING printed on it in bold type. Then, when they find themselves worrying, I suggest they take it out and use it as a trigger to stop their negative thought processes, and to replace them by prayer. Paul's advice is to "tell God your needs." This means that we should spell out to God in as much detail as possible the ramifications of the problem. The secret is simple—we replace worry by telling God about it, and then trust Him to take care of the problem.

Lord, on the surface, this sounds a bit simplistic, but help me to have an increasing confidence in the power of Your Word as I share it with the next worrier I meet—perhaps today. Amen.

We replace worry by telling God about it.

# YOU'RE AN ANGEL

"Elijah was afraid and ran for his life. When he came to Beersheba in Judah, he left his servant there, while he himself went a day's journey into the desert. He came to a broom tree, sat down under it and prayed that he might die. 'I have had enough, LORD' he said. 'Take my life; I am no better than my ancestors.' *Then he lay down under the tree and fell asleep. All at once an angel touched him* and said, 'Get up and eat.' He looked around, and there by his head was a cake of bread baked over hot coals, and a jar of water. He ate and drank and then lay down again."

1 Kings 19:3–6

On this last day of a week in which we have been looking at some specific problems which people face, I am going to invite you to look with me at the passage before us in order to see how the angel of the Lord ministered and cared for Elijah.

## Elijah and the Angel of the Lord

When Queen Jezebel became incensed against Elijah, he fled into the desert, became extremely disconsolate and discouraged, and begged God to take his life. Notice how the angel of the Lord dealt with Elijah and his problem. First, he focused on Elijah's physical needs: Elijah was given food, drink, and a chance to rest. Second, he was given an opportunity to get things off his chest, so to speak. Talking, as we have seen, is therapeutic. The more Elijah talked, the more he aired his problem and so brought about a release of his pent-up emotions. Third, the Lord set about challenging and redirecting Elijah's thinking, showing him that he was not alone or in danger of death. Elijah's problem was twofold: he was overstretched (hence the food, drink, and rest), and he was the victim of wrong thinking. The Lord taught Elijah how to think differently—a basic principle in effective caring—and, before long, Elijah was back in contact with people, free from his doubt and depression.

The angel of the Lord, in this story, presents a good model for Christian caring. We must encourage people to get physical help if they need it, urge them to express their feelings, and help them to think more clearly and more in line with what God thinks. Such a ministry is not reserved for angels. It can become your ministry as well.

O God, I never cease to be amazed at how You speak to me through Your Word. I desire a ministry such as the angel had when caring for Elijah. Now that I have discovered it, help me to develop it. For Your own dear name's sake. Amen.

Such a ministry is not reserved for angels.

We can help the other person to put his wounds in the context of Christ's wounds, linking our little pains with the great suffering of God in Christ. This will not take the pain away; but it will make it more bearable.

— Frank Wright

_____

_____

_____

_____

_____

_____

_____

_____

_____

_____

_____

_____

_____

_____

_____

_____

_____

_____

_____

_____

_____

# Journal Entry

# WEEK 6

# CARING
# FOR
# YOURSELF

God's love within us

even gives us the right to

forgive ourselves. It gives

us the power as well.

# BALANCED CARING

"Hearing that Jesus had silenced the Sadducees, the Pharisees got together. One of them, an expert in the law, tested him with this question: 'Teacher, which is the greatest commandment in the Law?' Jesus replied: '"Love the Lord your God with all you heart and with all your soul and with all your mind." This is the first and greatest commandment. And the second is like it: *"Love your neighbor as yourself."* All the Law and the Prophets hang on these two commandments.'"

## Matthew 22:34–40

If we are to care effectively for others, we must learn how to care for ourselves. This week, therefore, we turn to examine this important issue.

## Self-love and Love of Self

Some people think that Christianity teaches that they must love others but not themselves. This is a mistake. Christianity teaches self-love: "Love your neighbor *as* yourself." Notice that I use the word *self-love* and not *love of self.* The two are quite different. Love of self is egocentric interest; self-love is healthy personal concern. If you do not love yourself, you would not develop yourself. Those who love others and not themselves, allowing others to sap the life out of them, end up in disaster. On the other hand, as we have seen, if one organizes life around the self and becomes self-centered, then that, too, ends in disaster.

The words, "Love your neighbor as yourself," show that we are to be balanced in our caring. You are to care for others as you care for yourself, and you are to care for yourself as you care for others. This saves the caring from being one-sided: caring for others and neglecting yourself, or caring for yourself and neglecting others. I know many Christians who focus on caring for others but who do not have a healthy and balanced concern for themselves. And what happens? In most cases they end up needing the help and attention of others because they are overspent. Look at the life of Jesus. Does He ever appear on the pages of the Gospels as overspent? Tired, yes; weary, yes—but not overspent. His regard for others was balanced by a healthy regard for Himself.

O Father, help me to be a well-adjusted person, so that all my virtues are balanced, for I know that unbalanced virtues can make me lopsided. Amen.

Christianity teaches self-love.

# A HEALTHY
# SELF-CONCEPT

"What I tell you in the dark, speak in the daylight;
what is whispered in your ear, proclaim from the housetops.
Do not be afraid of those who kill the body but cannot kill
the soul. Rather, be afraid of the one who can destroy both
soul and body in hell. Are not two sparrows sold for a penny?
Yet not one of them will fall to the ground apart from the will
of your Father. And even the very hairs of your head are all
numbered. So don't be afraid; *you are worth more than
many sparrows.*"

## Matthew 10:27–31

We said yesterday that before we can effectively care for
others we must learn how to care for ourselves. Caring for
ourselves will not weaken or diminish our care for others;
rather, it will strengthen it.

## Valued by God

We ask ourselves: What steps do we need to take to
develop a healthy self-love? The first step is to *build a proper
self-image or self-concept.* What is our self-concept? It is the
image we carry of ourselves deep down in our hearts. And
this self-image is the most determinative part of our
personality. You tell me the way you see yourself, and I can

almost predict the course of your life, because you will act and behave in harmony with that self-image. If you see yourself as worthless, inferior, or inadequate, this is the way you will act in your relationships. If, however, you see yourself as a person of inestimable worth, someone who was redeemed at history's highest cost, the blood of Christ, then you will move through the world with the deep conviction that you are of value to Him and to His universe.

Permit a personal testimony here. For much of my life (up until my early thirties), I had a very negative view of myself. I felt I wasn't worth very much, and thus my ministry was motivated to increase my feelings of self-worth by what I did for others. I tried to get people to like me, and when they didn't, I was shattered. Then I locked on to this concept that I was of great worth to God, and I didn't have to work to get people to like me: *He* liked me. That was enough. Since then, reinforced by this inner conviction, I am free to give to others without wanting something in return. I have all I want—God *loves* me.

O Father, cleanse my self-concept this day so that I see myself as a person of worth and value to You. Then I shall move out to care for others from a position of strength and not weakness. I shall be a giver—not a getter. Thank You, Father. Amen.

Self-image is the most determinative part of our personality.

# THE GLORY OF GOD

"Do you not know that your bodies are members of Christ himself? Shall I then take the members of Christ and unite them with a prostitute? Never! Do you not know that he who unites himself with a prostitute is one with her in body? For it is said, 'The two will become one flesh.' But he who unites himself with the Lord is one with him in spirit. Flee from sexual immorality. All other sins a man commits are outside his body, but he who sins sexually sins against his own body. *Do you not know that your body is a temple of the Holy Spirit,* who is in you, whom you have received from God? You are not your own; you were bought at a price. Therefore honor God with your body."

## 1 Corinthians 6:15–20

We continue meditating on the need to care for ourselves. Yesterday we said that the first step to take in caring for ourselves is to develop a healthy self-concept. The way we see ourselves determines the way we relate to ourselves and to others. The second step is this—*pay careful attention to your physical functioning.* Do you eat, rest, exercise, and relax properly? Your body is a temple of the Holy Spirit; if you don't treat His temple right, how can you treat others right?

## Care for the Physical Body

When I was a young Christian, I used to think that Paul's words "our vile body" in Philippians 3:21 (KJV) meant that we were to treat our bodies with contempt, until someone showed me that the word *vile* meant "lowly," and Paul was comparing the present body with the new body we shall have one day in the future.

Many Christians regard the physical body as an encumbrance or a hindrance. It is not. God has given us our bodies for a purpose, and we need to treat them with the greatest respect. Every meal should be a sacrament, offered on the altar of fitter living and finer possibilities. If you eat to excess, you will end up with excess baggage, which will overburden your heart. A spare tire around your waistline is not a life saver but a life destroyer. Exercise is important, too. God made your body to *move*—make sure it does. You must not forget rest or relaxation either. If you don't rest and relax properly, the instrument of your spirit (the body) will be less than effective. Whether you eat or drink, said the apostle Paul, do all for the glory of God (1 Cor. 10:31)—and the glory of God dwells in a physically fit person.

My Lord and my God, I am seeing that
I can't care effectively for others until I learn how
to care for myself. Help me to be a good tenant
of Your temple. For Jesus' sake. Amen.

God has given us our bodies for a purpose.

# TAKE TIME
# TO BE ALONE

"But when you pray, do not be like the hypocrites, for they love to pray standing in the synagogues and on the street corners to be seen by men. I tell you the truth, they have received their reward in full. *When you pray, go into your room, close the door* and pray to your Father, who is unseen. Then your Father, who sees what is done in secret, will reward you. And when you pray, do not keep on babbling like pagans, for they think they will be heard because of their many words. Do not be like them, for your Father knows what you need before you ask him."

## Matthew 6:5–8

We are looking at some of the steps we need to take in order to care for ourselves effectively. If we fail to develop a healthy self-love, we will not be able to develop a healthy love for others. The third step to take is this—*build into your daily schedule a time (or times) when you can be alone.*

## Time with God

Some of the time you spend alone, you will want to spend with God. Don't fool yourself into thinking that you don't need to get alone with God at a particular time, in a particular place, because you can find God all the time and everywhere. If you are to find God all the time, you must find Him sometime; and if you are to find Him everywhere, you must find Him somewhere. When you spend time alone with God, make sure you have your Bible with you. Read it in His presence, and you will find that the God who spoke through those words thousands of years ago speaks through them still.

You need time alone not only to make contact with God but just to relax. You might want to spend time relaxing by reading a book or going for a walk. I come across many people on my travels who tell me that they feel guilty about having time to themselves (other than their prayer time) because there are so many needs to be met. If you feel guilty about having time to yourself, this is a pretty good indication that your self-concept needs attention. Jesus took time away from the crowds (and sometimes His disciples) to be alone. It is not true that the harder you drive yourself, the more you can accomplish. You can learn to accomplish more by doing less. And one way to do so is by taking time off—even if this puts you temporarily out of contact with people who need help.

Father, I see that taking time off need not
be selfish but prudent, for such times give me
a new perspective on caring. Help me to organize
my life so I can accomplish more—without
frenzied activity. For Jesus' sake. Amen.

You can learn to accomplish more by doing less.

# Stay In Your Circle

*"I will praise the LORD, who counsels me; even at night my heart instructs me.* I have set the Lord always before me. Because he is at my right hand, I will not be shaken. Therefore my heart is glad and my tongue rejoices; my body also will rest secure, because you will not abandon me to the grave, nor will you let your Holy One see decay. You have made known to me the path of life; you will fill me with joy in your presence, with eternal pleasures at your right hand."

Psalm 16:7–11

Today we examine the fourth step we need to take if we are to care for ourselves effectively—*recognize your limitations and don't go beyond them.*

## Everything God Asks Me To

Many people tend to push themselves, or allow others to push them, beyond the boundaries of their humanity or experience. I have discovered that people who allow themselves to be easily manipulated have one stock verse: "I can do everything through him who gives me strength" (Phil. 4:13). Now I am the last one to discourage anyone from setting their sights on higher goals, or from reaching out to achieve greater things (as editions of *Every Day with*

*Jesus* will show), but we must interpret Paul's words correctly. The Living Bible paraphrase, in my view, brings out the truth of the original Greek most expertly: "I can do everything God asks me to with the help of Christ who gives me the strength and power." "Everything God asks me to"—that is the secret. Some people fail to realize this and think they are obliged to respond to every call and demand that comes their way. Often this attitude comes from a wrong self-concept, where the person sees himself as unworthy or inferior, and has to compensate for that by trying harder.

We need to realize and understand that God has a circle, so to speak, for each one of us in which we can best function for Him. When we stay inside that circle, we achieve what I often refer to as "maximum effectiveness with minimum weariness." Outside of that circle, however, we achieve maximum weariness with minimum effectiveness. Some of us may have a little way to go before we get to the edge of our circle, but we must be careful we are never pushed beyond it.

Gracious Father, help me to be aware of my limitations and not allow myself to be driven or pushed beyond them. Help me to be the person You want me to be. In Jesus' Name. Amen.

Help me to be aware of my limitations.

# DO IT GENTLY

"This is how we know what love is: Jesus Christ laid down his life for us. And we ought to lay down our lives for our brothers. If anyone has material possessions and sees his brother in need but has no pity on him, how can the love of God be in him? Dear children, let us not love with words or tongue but with actions and in truth. This then is how we know that we belong to the truth, and how we set our hearts at rest in his presence whenever our hearts condemn us. *For God is greater than our hearts, and he knows everything.*"

## 1 John 3:16–20

A fifth step that we can take in order to care for ourselves is this—*be gentle with yourself whenever you fail or make a mistake*. Some Christians have such a harsh set of attitudes that whenever they fail in anything, or make a mistake, they come down on themselves with a heavy hand of judgment. They reprimand themselves so severely that an atmosphere of gloom and depression fills the soul. When Christians become depressed or dejected following a failure or a mistake, it is usually a good sign that they are judging themselves more harshly than they ought. I am not talking here about sin, but about slips, foibles, and mistakes.

## Loving Self-Correction

In a healthy personality where self-love is understood and practiced, whenever such people make a mistake, they will evaluate themselves and their actions in a gentle and loving way. They will feel a degree of disappointment, but they will not be desolated by it; they will feel shaken but not shattered. Those who are overwhelmed by their mistakes are using a set of mechanisms in their personality that do not come from God but from their past experiences and relationships.

What does the Scripture say? "For if our heart condemn us, God is greater than our heart" (1 John 3:20 KJV). How does God deal with us when we make a mistake? Gently. The Psalmist said, "Thy gentleness hath made me great" (Ps. 18:35 KJV). God loves you too much either to over-discipline you or underdiscipline you. You must love yourself in the same way. But one more thing: do you congratulate and compliment the people you love when they have done something well? Then do the same for yourself. You care for others—care for yourself, too.

O Father, help me to see myself as You see me— a person of worth, even when I have made a mistake; and help me to be as gentle with myself as You are with me. In Jesus' name I pray. Amen.

You care for others—care for yourself too.

# BEING A
# LOVE RECEIVER

"We know that we live in him and he in us, because he has given us of his Spirit. And we have seen and testify that the Father has sent his Son to be the Savior of the world. If anyone acknowledges that Jesus is the Son of God, God lives in him and he in God. And so we know and rely on the love God has for us. God is love. Whoever lives in love lives in God, and God in him. Love is made complete among us so that we will have confidence on the day of judgment, because in this world we are like him. *There is no fear in love. But perfect love drives out fear*, because fear has to do with punishment. The man who fears is not made perfect in love. We loved because he first loved us."

## 1 John 4:13–19

We now come to a final day of a week in which we have been looking at some of the steps we need to take in order to care for ourselves. Today we look at the sixth step—*learn to receive love whenever it is offered to you from others.* I say *learn* because many are able to *give* love, but they are unable to *receive* it.

## Feelings About Being Loved

A friend once said to me, "Why is it that I find it easy to love, but whenever people love me I become strangely embarrassed?" There are many reasons for this. One is that such a person may not have received much love in childhood and so has never learned how to cope with those positive feelings. Perhaps people were criticized more than they were praised, rejected more than accepted, and so they learned to cope with those negative feelings more easily than with the positive ones. Thus, when love is shown, the feelings it arouses are difficult to handle, and the person becomes embarrassed.

Another reason is due to what one writer calls "a fear of love." All of us, deep down, long to be loved, to be protected, to be cared for; but to experience such love, or to express it in return, can be threatening. When people get to know us intimately, they will get to know our weaknesses. There is always the possibility that they will reject us because of these weaknesses. So to protect ourselves from possible rejection, we maintain our distance and subtly push them away. To overcome this fear, we must learn to let others love us, open ourselves to them, and take the risk of being hurt. We will remain stunted and dwarfed in our personalities if we only give love and do not receive it. We must learn not only to love but also to let others love us.

Gracious and loving heavenly Father,
help me overcome any difficulties I may have
in receiving love. I know it is risky opening
my heart to others, but if I am to grow, then
I must learn to do this. Help me Lord Jesus,
for Your own name's sake. Amen.

We must learn to let others love us.

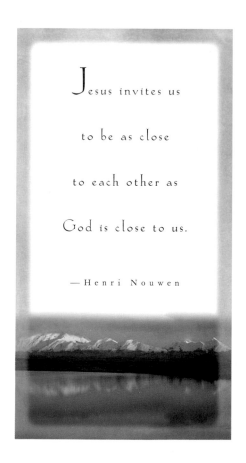

Jesus invites us

to be as close

to each other as

God is close to us.

— Henri Nouwen

# Journal Entry

_____

_____

_____

_____

_____

_____

_____

_____

_____

_____

_____

_____

_____

_____

_____

_____

_____

_____

_____

_____

_____

_____

_____

_____

_____

_____

_____

_____

_____

_____

_____

_____

_____

_____

_____

_____

_____

_____

_____

_____

_____

_____

_____

_____

# PITFALLS AND DANGERS

Understanding

is sometimes better

than advice.

— Larry Crabb

# MANIPULATION

"As Jesus started on his way, a man ran up to him and fell on his knees before him. 'Good teacher,' he asked, 'what must I do to inherit eternal life?' 'Why do you call me good?' Jesus answered. 'No one is good—except God alone. You know the commandments: "Do not murder, do not commit adultery, do not steal, do not give false testimony, do not defraud, honor your father and mother."' 'Teacher,' he declared, 'all these I have kept since I was a boy.' Jesus looked at him and loved him. 'One thing you lack,' he said. 'Go, sell everything you have and give to the poor, and you will have treasure in heaven. Then come, follow me.' *At this the man's face fell. He went away sad, because he had great wealth.*"

## Mark 10:17–22

The ministry of caring, like all other ministries, has its own pitfalls and dangers. This week we shall examine together some of the perils we face when we set about the task of bearing one another's burdens and so fulfilling the law of Christ.

## Freedom to Accept or Reject

The first pitfall we shall examine is that of *manipulation*. We manipulate people when we try to control them and deny them their freedom. When attempting to help someone, you may long to see them act upon your suggestions or implement your advice. You may grieve profoundly when they take an opposite direction, but you must never, never, never try to control that person, or dominate him to the degree that he loses his freedom. To do so violates a person's autonomy and ignores the fact that every person is a volitional being, made in the image of God.

In the passage before us today, Jesus is seen sharing the principles of eternal life with the rich young ruler. The young man was only a step away from the kingdom of God but was unable to commit himself. "He went sadly away, for he was very rich." Jesus was undoubtedly impressed by this young man's personality and character, for the verse says: "Jesus looked at him and loved him" (v. 21). Notice, however, that Jesus' love for this young man did not lead Him to violate the man's freedom. The Master made no move to remonstrate with him, plead with him, or denounce him for resisting His message. He gave him the freedom to accept or reject it. He loved him enough to respect his freedom. And so must you love people in this way. The caring ministry is not a power struggle. You are not there to prove something. You are there to care.

Gracious Father, I see the pitfalls. Help me to be free from power struggles as I develop this ministry of caring. I don't want to control people: I want to care for them. Amen.

Jesus loved him enough to respect his freedom.

# CURB YOUR
# CURIOSITY

*See to it, brothers, that none of you has a sinful, unbelieving heart that turns away from the living God.* But encourage one another daily, as long as it is called Today, so that none of you may be hardened by sin's deceitfulness. We have come to share in Christ if we hold firmly till the end the confidence we had at first. As has just been said: 'Today, if you hear his voice, do not harden your hearts as you did in the rebellion.' Who were they who heard and rebelled? Were they not all those Moses led out of Egypt? And with whom was he angry for forty years? Was it not with those who sinned, whose bodies fell in the desert? And to whom did God swear that they would never enter his rest if not to those who disobeyed?

## Hebrews 3:12–18

We said yesterday that the ministry of caring, like all other ministries, has its pitfalls and dangers. We saw the danger in manipulating people, and asked God to help make us carers, not controllers. Today we examine another pitfall—*overcuriosity*.

## Setting Boundaries

Caring, as we have seen, involves a high degree of closeness and intimacy. Sometimes it involves talking about deep personal problems, such as one's attitudes, basic needs, and inner feelings. Be careful that you don't become involved in probing a person for information simply to satiate your own curiosity. I know hundreds of people whose ministry of caring has been ruined because they allowed themselves to go beyond the bounds of propriety in their questioning, and sought to meet their own needs rather than the needs of the person they were supposed to be helping.

If you fail to recognize that caring can make you vulnerable to your own sinful tendencies and fantasies, and you do not throw yourself in complete dependency upon the Holy Spirit for assistance, then you might hurt more people than you help. This is why, when intimate things have to be shared, such as a person's inner feelings or sexual needs, it is prudent for men to help men and women to help women. Sometimes this rule can be waived (as in the case of a minister or a professional counselor), but generally it is a good rule to follow. The same Holy Spirit who motivates you to care can protect you from becoming overcurious or voyeuristic. But be watchful that your tendencies do not lead you into areas you should not go. Commit yourself daily to the Holy Spirit's control and protection.

O God, give me a clear insight to see
into my own heart, for I may be cloaking my own
curiosity with the garments of caring. If so, then
deal with my heart in the way You know best.
For Jesus' sake. Amen.

Commit yourself daily to the Holy Spirit's control and protection.

# DISCIPLINED DESIRES

"I thank God, whom I serve, as my forefathers did, with a clear conscience, as night and day I constantly remember you in my prayers. Recalling your tears, I long to see you, so that I may be filled with joy. I have been reminded of your sincere faith, which first lived in your grandmother Lois and in your mother Eunice and, I am persuaded, now lives in you also. For this reason I remind you to fan into flame the gift of God, which is in you through the laying on of my hands. *For God did not give us a spirit of timidity, but a spirit of power, of love and of self-discipline.*"

## 2 Timothy 1:3—7

Today we examine another danger that can confront us when we become involved in the caring ministry—*caring when care is not needed.*

## Overenthusiasm

When I was in my teens, a friend of mine underwent a training program with the St. John Ambulance Society. After becoming qualified, he spent most of his time searching for people whom he could help. When he couldn't find any, he persuaded people who didn't have genuine problems that they needed his expert care and attention. I saw several of my friends walking around with bandaged limbs when there was really nothing wrong with them! When he found a genuine reason to care, he went at it with more enthusiasm than was good or necessary. A scratch required a tourniquet, a simple wrist sprain was supported by an arm sling! After a while, his overenthusiasm became widely known, and people avoided him as they would a plague.

Now it is possible that these meditations on this subject of caring will cause you to become more concerned than you have ever been before about the need to help your brothers and sisters who may be hurting. However, I beg you, make sure the people you try to help really need it, and are not just objects on whom you can try out your new ideas and skills. The desire you have to help others is good, but you need more than desire—you must have disciplined desire. Desire is the driving force that moves us forward in life, but desire has to be controlled by discipline. So be firm with yourself. If my emphasis on discipline sounds like a diminution rather than an augmentation of the ministry of caring, it is not. Discipline is as necessary to effective Christian living as wings are to a bird!

My Lord and my God, help me to harness all my desires so that they work in the most productive and beneficial ways. This I ask in Jesus' name. Amen.

Desire has to be controlled by discipline.

# CARE — ONE AT A TIME!

"My son, if you accept my words and store up my commands within you, turning your ear to wisdom and applying your heart to understanding, and if you call out for insight and cry aloud for understanding, and if you look for it as for silver and search for it as for hidden treasure, then you will understand the fear of the LORD and find the knowledge of God. For the LORD gives wisdom and from his mouth come knowledge and understanding. He holds victory in store for the upright, he is a shield to those whose walk is blameless, for he guards the course of the just and protects the way of his faithful ones. *Then you will understand what is right and just and fair—every good path.*"

Proverbs 2:1–9

As we continue our investigation into the dangers and pitfalls that confront us in the caring ministry, today we examine the danger of *caring for too many at one time.*

## Good Advice

Gary Collins, a Christian psychologist, says, "Most of us have had the experience of reading articles or listening to speakers who dramatically picture human needs, and then challenge us to reach out in ways that will eliminate injustice or change the world. Such pleas can arouse considerable guilt, followed by frustration because there seems so little any one person can really do." Wise words.

I cautioned you yesterday on the danger of over-enthusiasm, and today I utter a similar caution—care for one person at a time. Later on, of course, when you have gained greater experience and understanding, then the circle of your caring can be widened. It is good advice, I believe, to begin by caring for one person—and one only. No one has been given a responsibility to care for the whole world. Our task is to care for the person near us who is in need. Jesus helped people one at a time. There were occasions certainly when He preached to the multitudes and fed the thousands, but someone has pointed out that, in the Gospels, there are no fewer than nineteen *private* conferences that Jesus had with people, thus illustrating the importance of helping people one at a time. Again, I say, don't let the enthusiasm of the moment lead you into caring for more than one person at a time. You will not be able to care for everyone, but you will be able to care for someone.

Father, thank You for reminding me that
the way to care for people is to care for them
one at a time. Help me to see the wisdom of this
and not to take on more than You would
have me to. In Jesus' Name. Amen.

You will not be able to care for everyone.

# CARING FOR THE FAMILY

"Treat younger men as brothers, older women as mothers, and younger women as sisters with absolute purity. Give proper recognition to those widows who are really in need. But if a widow has children or grandchildren, these should learn first of all to put their religion into practice by caring for their own family and so repaying their parents and grandparents, for this is pleasing to God. The widow who is really in need and left all alone puts her hope in God and continues night and day to pray and to ask God for help. But the widow who lives for pleasure is dead even while she lives. Give the people these instructions, too, so that no one may be open to blame. *If anyone does not provide for his relatives, and especially for his immediate family, he has denied the faith and is worse than an unbeliever.*"

1 Timothy 5:1–8

Today we look at one of the most serious of all the pitfalls that confront us in the caring ministry—*caring for others to the detriment of our own families.* Sometimes this happens in the homes of ministers, who allow the demands of their ministry to erode away any time spent with the family. There have been several professional men with whom I have been in contact over the years (ministers, doctors, and counselors) whose marriages were breaking up because they spent little or no time with their families. "Nothing is so pathetic," said one writer, "than a dedicated Christian who has become so concerned in caring for other people that he or she has forgotten the family and lost the respect of people at home."

This is a tendency that I have had to watch all of my life, and sadly I have to confess that at times I have not been too successful at it. It is so easy to get involved in speaking and writing (even writing an *Every Day with Jesus* on caring!) and miss out on one of life's most important ministries— caring for one's family.

## God's Scale of Values

If God permitted me to have my life over again, I would concentrate on giving equal if not more time to my family than I would give to the church. This is not to downgrade the importance of the church or to deny its place in the world. The church has been my life, my joy, my support, but I have come to see, over the years, that the home has almost as high a priority as the church in God's scale of values. An institution that is mentioned in all sixty-six books of the Bible must be of supreme importance.

Father, I see so clearly that it is inconsistent
to care for people outside the home but not to care
for those within it. You who created both family
and church, help me to make sure the family
is my highest priority. Amen.

One of life's most important ministries—caring for one's family.

# BODY CARE

"Peter was kept in prison, but *the church was earnestly praying to God for him.* The night before Herod was to bring him to trial, Peter was sleeping between two soldiers, bound with two chains, and sentries stood guard at the entrance. Suddenly an angel of the Lord appeared and a light shone in the cell. He struck Peter on the side and woke him up. 'Quick, get up!' he said, and the chains fell off Peter's wrists. Then the angel said to him, 'Put on your clothes and sandals.' And Peter did so. 'Wrap your cloak around you and follow me,' the angel told him. Peter followed him out of the prison, but he had no idea that what the angel was doing was really happening; he thought he was seeing a vision."

## Acts 12:5–9

Today we consider the last of the perils which can confront us when we undertake a ministry of caring—*caring without making sure of spiritual back-up and support.*

## Spiritual Backup

There is no such thing as *do-it-yourself* Christianity. The message of the New Testament is that Christians should link themselves with other Christians so that they can give one another prayer and spiritual support. There used to be an advertisement on television some years ago, sponsored by a number of insurance companies, which said: "You need the strength of the insurance company wrapped around you."

This would be my message to all those who want to discover life's greatest purpose and move out into the ministry of caring for which God has designed them—you need the strength of the church wrapped around you.

Don't try to care for others without making sure that you have some strong spiritual backup in the prayers of the church or at least a group in the church. From time to time, you need people not only to pray for you but to pray with you. There will be times of failure, discouragement, and difficulty when the prayers of a close-knit group or fellowship can make all the difference. However, you might say, "In my church no one seems that concerned about others." Is that really so, I wonder? Perhaps there are others, like you, who long for the support of a small group as they exercise their own individual caring ministry. It's not too much to conclude that an omnipotent God can also lead you to others who can give and receive the support which enhances your effectiveness in the body of Christ.

My Father and my God, deepen my conviction that You are a prayer-answering God, and place me alongside those whom I can support and who can support me in this vital ministry of caring. For Your own dear name's sake. Amen.

There is no such thing as *do-it-yourself* Christianity.

# HE'S MY BROTHER

"Keep on loving each other as brothers. Do not forget to entertain strangers, for by so doing some people have entertained angels without knowing it. Remember those in prison as if you were their fellow prisoners, and those who are mistreated as if you yourselves were suffering. Marriage should be honored by all, and the marriage bed kept pure, for God will judge the adulterer and all the sexually immoral. Keep your lives free from the love of money and be content with what you have, because God has said, 'Never will I leave you; never will I forsake you.' So we say with confidence, 'The Lord is my helper; I will not be afraid. What can man do to me?'"

## Hebrews 13:1—6

We come now to the last day on this series of meditations on the subject of discovering life's greatest purpose. What is that purpose? To love God and care for others. Just as I was about to write this last page—a page on which I planned to share a final thought on caring—an old friend telephoned me for a few minutes' chat. During the course of the conversation, I mentioned that I was writing the last page of this study, and he enquired as to the theme I had chosen. I said, "The ministry of caring." After a few moments' silence, he said, "Caring is carrying." I asked him to explain what he meant, and he told me this story—a story I feel sure you must have heard—but I was strangely moved to scrap my original idea for this page and to include the story as a final illustration and comment.

## He's Not Heavy

A girl was seen carrying her little brother home after he had fallen and cut his knee. The little boy was almost as big as she, and as she seemed to be laboring under the burden of his weight, a neighbor said, "Put him down, my dear. He's too heavy for you to carry." The little girl replied, somewhat indignantly, "He's not heavy; he's my brother."

Yes, caring is carrying. Look around you, and you will see that some of your brothers and sisters are hurt and wounded. Remember, they are part of your family—the family of God. Your Father would have you reach out to them and help them. He provides special power for the task. Caring is carrying: and when others try to deter you and say that your burden is too heavy for you, strengthened by the knowledge that you are both your Father's children, you will say, "He's no burden; he's my brother."

Gracious God and loving heavenly Father, thank you for challenging me during these meditations. May every day of my life be employed in fulfilling life's greatest purpose—loving You and caring for others. In Jesus' name I pray. Amen.

Caring is carrying.

God is a
compassionate God.
This means, first of all,
that he has chosen
to be God-with-us.
What really counts
is that in pain and
suffering someone
stays with us.

—Henri Nouwen